The Military Career of
Sir Howard Douglas

GENERAL SIR HOWARD DOUGLAS

The Military Career of Sir Howard Douglas

Gunner, Engineer and Wellington's Special Agent

S. W. Fullom

LEONAUR

The Military Career of Sir Howard Douglas
Gunner, Engineer and Wellington's Special Agent
by S. W. Fullom

FIRST EDITION

Leonaur is an imprint of Oakpast Ltd

ISBN: 978-1-78282-902-7 (hardcover)
ISBN: 978-1-78282-903-4 (softcover)

http://www.leonaur.com

Publisher's Notes

Contents

CHAPTER 1

The Father of Sir Howard Douglas

The name of Douglas is familiar to English ears, and none is more famous in Scotland. It has figured in tale and history there from the days of tradition, when we are told of its being won by the "black-grey man" who came to the rescue of the king's lieutenant in a battle with a pirate chief. Our own great poet has celebrated the

> *Renowned Douglas, whose high deeds,*
> *Whose hot incursions, and great name in arms,*
> *Holds from all soldiers chief majority,*
> *And military title capital,*
> *Through all the kingdoms that acknowledge Christ.*

And there is hardly one of Scotland's bards who has not touched on the same theme.

The family became allied to the Scottish crown by the marriage of the Lord of Dalkeith with the Lady Mary, fifth daughter of James I., and sister of James II.; and the latter monarch created his brother-in-law Earl of Morton. The title descended from father to son through three generations, when King James V. seized James, the third Earl, and imprisoned him in Inverness Castle until he consented to entail it on Robert Douglas of Lochlevin, whom the king wished to console for having a little disturbed his wedding by carrying off the bride.

But nothing was gained by the motion, as he died before the earl, and no sooner lay in his grave than Morton abjured the arrangement, and executed a new deed, entailing the title on the husband of his second daughter—James Douglas, brother of David Earl of Angus, and Lord Chancellor and Regent of Scotland during the minority of James VI.—who became fourth Earl of Morton. This nobleman was succeeded by his nephew, Archibald Douglas Earl of Angus, from

7

whom the title of Morton passed by the entail to William Douglas of Lochlevin, who was descended from the first Earl, and made the sixth inheritor of his honours.

Another sixth generation threatened the earldom with a new diversion, as it was now borne by an old man, apparently determined on dying a bachelor. But the twelfth hour brought him to better thoughts, and he fell in love with a beauty who enabled him to leave his title to a son. This shut out the next branch of the family, represented by young Charles Douglas, who had come almost within reach of the coronet, being the lineal descendant of Sir George Douglas of Kirkness, second son of Earl William of Lochlevin, and hence presumptive heir. But Fortune made up for the slip by designing him to win honours of his own; and these lost none of their lustre on descending to his son Howard Douglas, whose career forms the subject of this volume.

Charles Douglas ran his course in the navy, which he entered as a child, passing through the successive grades of rank until he appears in command of a frigate— at one time taking part in the naval operations on the coast of America during the War of Independence, and afterwards capturing prizes in the Channel. Subsequently he was employed in organising the navy of Russia, on the recommendation of the British Government; and he succeeded in placing it on a good footing, when he returned to England. His reputation now stood so high that the Admiralty selected him to command a squadron for the relief of Quebec, which the Americans had besieged, and were exerting every means to reduce.

Its capture would entail the loss of Canada if not of our whole dominion in America, and the public were in the greatest alarm at the danger, as the closing of the St. Lawrence seemed to cut off assistance. But the panic abated on the announcement that the succours to be sent out were intrusted to Captain Douglas, who was known to be familiar with the American waters, and had established a character for energy and action which inspired confidence. The general feeling is reflected in a letter addressed to him on the occasion by Lord Townshend.

His Lordship writes:

The day before I left town to bring my family out of the country, I asked either Lord George Germain or Lord Sandwich (I think it was the former) who went up the river with the relief?

and was told it was you. I replied, 'I am glad you have fixed on so good a man. You cannot inquire better upon all occasions after the River St. Lawrence than from him. He will tell you as much as Mr. Cooke (probably the celebrated Captain Cook), or anyone else.'

Captain Douglas worked day and night to hasten the equipment of the ships, and the Admiralty urged him to even greater exertion. Lord Sandwich writes:

For God's sake, get the *Isis* down to Blackstakes the next spring-tide, the First Lord. Your being ready to leave early in February is of the utmost importance to the public service. I think the fate of Quebec depends upon it.

The squadron sailed at the appointed time, and the beginning of April found it on the coast of Newfoundland, waiting for the breakup of the ice to make for the St. Lawrence. But Captain Douglas was not content to wait long. There seemed no prospect of the navigation opening, and he knew that Quebec must be in the last extremity, as it had now been invested some months, and subjected to repeated assaults. It occurred to him that he might drive his ship through the ice, and he took advantage of a rising gale to put her before the wind, and run against a block twelve feet thick as an experiment. The shock had a greater effect than he expected, crumbling the ice in pieces. In his despatch to Mr. Stephens, he says:

We now thought it an enterprise worthy of an English ship of the line in our king and country's sacred cause, and an effort due to the gallant defence of Quebec, to make the attempt of pressing her by force of sail through the thick, broad, and closely-connected fields of ice (as formidable as the Gulf of St. Lawrence ever exhibited), to which we saw no bounds.

The frozen tract was found to extend for sixty leagues; but he persevered in his design, undeterred by gales and snowstorms and innumerable perils and accidents, and nine days of unwearied labour brought the ship to open water. Here she was joined by the *Surprise* and *Martin*, which had followed in her track; and the little squadron Altered the St. Lawrence under a heavy fall of snow. On the 3rd of May it ran into the basin of Quebec, and was received with acclamations; the ships lowered their boats and landed the reinforcements under cover of their guns, while General Carleton made a sortie with the garrison, and drove the besiegers from their works. The siege was raised in an instant; the British flag waved over the heights, and Canada was saved.

The Americans still held Lake Champlain, where they kept a flotilla, which gave them command of the shore. But Captain Douglas considered his work but half done while they retained this advantage. He had brought from England the framework of a sloop prepared at his suggestion, and he put her together at St. John's, and launched her on the lake. She was armed with eighteen guns, and he provided her a consort in a schooner, carrying fourteen, and remarkable for her speed.

Both vessels were completed within six weeks; and his exertions were so unremitting that the same time sufficed to equip a flotilla equal to the enemy's, comprising thirty vessels mounting cannon, as many flat-bottomed boats, and a *gondola* of thirty tons, with four hundred *bateaux*. These he caused to be transported overland, then had them dragged up the rapids of Theresa and St. John's, and assembled them on the lake, under the command of Captain Pringle, who hoisted a commodore's pendant in the *Maria*, and advanced on the enemy.

The anxiety and harass of the undertaking were repaid by success. The American flotilla was brought to bay after a chase of several days, and every vessel destroyed, the few that escaped sinking being driven ashore. This victory cleared the lakes, and completed the liberation of Canada, which obtained for Captain Douglas the approbation of the king, who rewarded his services by the gift of a baronetcy.

The experience he acquired in the preparation of the flotilla developed a mechanical turn, and this led to his suggesting improvements in ships of war, both in equipment and construction. He originated the principle of a false keel, the use of locks, and the allotment of heavier guns to the quarter-deck of three-deckers—all of which were adopted by the Admiralty. (The facts are shown in a series of letters in the *Douglas Papers*, addressed to him by Sir Charles Middleton.)

His activity excited the wonder of his Russian friends, as they were aware that the death of a relative had brought him an independence, and he had refused the most tempting offers to remain in Russia. Admiral Greig writes to him from St. Petersburg in 1777:

I have just been dining with Count Panim, who inquired after you with professions of great esteem and regard. He said he was surprised to find that you still served at home, after having declined service here, from the easy and affluent fortune bequeathed to you. I told him I did not imagine any change of fortune or circumstances would make you decline the service of your native country, whenever your services were required.

His friend had justly estimated his character, for the sequel proved that he was now only in the middle of his career. On the 23rd of July, 1778, he commanded the *Stirling Castle* in Admiral Keppel's engagement with the French fleet under Count d'Orvilliers, and went into action with the van. But that engagement opened no way to distinction, and it was not till he was appointed Captain of the Fleet to Sir George Rodney that he found an opportunity of displaying his genius. The fleet of Count de Grasse came in sight on the 8th of April, 1782, and kept the British admiral to leeward for three days, though he exerted all his seamanship to bring on an action.

Maintaining the chase, his fast sailers drew so near, that they compelled De Grasse to relinquish the weather-gauge; but hardly had he done so, when a change of wind gave it to him again, and Rodney perceived that he must either engage him to leeward or allow him to escape. There could be no doubt as to the course for a British Admiral in such a situation, and a signal from the *Formidable* directed the *Marlborough* to lead along the lee of the French line, with the view of bringing on a general action.

The *Marlborough* was followed by the van of the British squadron, until it became apparent that the course of the *Formidable* pointed directly through an opening in the centre of the French fleet. This suggested to Sir Charles Douglas one of the boldest manoeuvres ever practised in naval warfare, and he urged the admiral to cut the enemy's line in two by piercing his centre. The incident is related in a letter from Admiral Sir Charles Dashwood in the *Douglas Papers*. (The letter has been printed in Sir Howard Douglas's *Naval Evolutions*):

I shall simply relate facts, to which I was an eyewitness, and can vouch for their truth. Being one of the *aides-de-camp* to the commander-in-chief on that memorable day, it was my duty to attend both on him and the captain of the fleet, as occasion might require. It so happened that sometime after the battle had commenced, and whilst we were warmly engaged, I was standing near Sir Charles Douglas, who was leaning on the hammocks (which in those days were stowed across the fore part of the quarterdeck), his head resting on one hand, and his eye occasionally glancing on the enemy's line, and apparently in deep meditation as if some great event was crossing his mind. Suddenly raising his head, and turning quickly round, he said, 'Dash! where's Sir George?'

'In the after-cabin, sir,' I replied.

He immediately went aft; I followed, and, on meeting Sir George coming from the cabin close to the wheel, he took off his cocked-hat with his right hand, holding his long spy-glass in his left, making a low and profound bow, said, 'Sir George, I give you joy of the victory.' 'Poll!' said the chief, as if half-angry, 'the day is not half won yet.'

'Break the line, Sir George,' said Sir Charles; 'the day is your own, and I will insure you the victory.'

'No,' said the admiral, 'I will not break any line.'

After another request, and another refusal, Sir Charles desired the helm to be put a-port: Sir George ordered it to starboard. On Sir Charles ordering it again to port, the admiral sternly said, 'Remember, Sir Charles, that I am commander-in-chief; starboard, sir,' addressing the master, who, during the controversy, had placed the helm amidships. The admiral and the captain then separated; the former going aft, and the latter forward. In the course of a couple of minutes or so, each turned and again met on the same spot, when Sir Charles quietly and coolly again addressed the chief,—'Only break the line, Sir George, and the day is your own!'

The admiral then said in a quick and hurried way, 'Well, well— do as you like,' and immediately turned round and walked into the after-cabin. The words 'Port the helm' were scarcely uttered when Sir Charles ordered me down with directions to commence firing on the larboard side. On my return to the quarter-deck I found the *Formidable* passing between two French ships, each nearly touching us. We were followed by the *Namur* and the rest of the ships astern; and from that moment the victory was decided in our favour."

★★★★★★

The occurrence is thus narrated by Admiral Count Bouet Willaumez, in *Batailles de Terre et de Mer*.)

"*C'est le 12 Avril, 1782, que les deux flottes se rencontrent par une brise variable de l'est au sud-sud-est; la flotte Française court babord amures, mais mal formée, et présente des lacunes dans sa ligne; la flotte*

12

Anglaise l'attcint par sous le vent, à contre-bord, et son avant-garde prolonge les vaisseaux Français àk distance; mais, au moment où le vaisseau le Formidable, monté par Rodney, atteint la flotte Française pour la prolonger à son tour comme a fait l'avant-garde Anglaise, le vent fraîchit un peu et adonne de deux quarts: 'Serrez le vent,' dit le Capitaine Douglas, flag-captain de Rodney, au master, qui tenait la barre du gouvernail: Rodney veut d'abord contrarier cet ordre; mais reconnaissant ensuite qu'il va lui permettre de couper la ligne Française et de la mettre en désordre, peut-être même entre deux feux, il s'écrie, au dire de l'historien Anglais Ekins, 'Then do it as you please!' (Faites donc comme il vous plaira!) Et cependant, dans ce hasard du vent, dans ces trois mots du Capitaine Douglas, mots incompris d'abord de Rodney, il y avait tout un nouveau système de combats de mer; bientôt, en effet, les vaisseaux Anglais le Formidable, l'Agamemnon, le Duke, &c., coupent la ligne Française et se répandent, les uns au large, les autres le long des vaisseaux Français, qu'ils mettent entre deux feux; le contre-amiral commandant l'arrière-garde Anglaise, imitant la manoeuvre de Rodney, vient, toujours à contre-bord, couper de nouveau notre ligne après le dernier vaisseau de notre avant-garde: en vain De Grasse multiplie ses signaux pour masser au combat sa ligne désemparée et coupée en trois tronçons; il est trop tard, la fumée empêche de voir les signaux."

★★★★★★

Little is known of Sir Charles Douglas's domestic life during this period, except that he married a foreign lady, who died about 1770, after she had borne him two sons and a daughter. He subsequently married Miss Wood, the daughter of an old Yorkshire family, and this union brought him another son, born at Gosport on the 23rd of January, 1776, and who received the baptismal name of Howard.

Howard Douglas had reached his third year when he sustained the greatest bereavement that can befall a child, in the death of his mother, though the loss was alleviated by the care of his aunt Helena, wife of James Baillie, Esq., of Olive Bank, near Musselburg. To her care he was now confided, together with his sister and half-brother Charles, and she became the centre of his early recollections. Such a character might leave an impression on natures of the sternest mould, and it is not surprising that one so warm-hearted remembered her fondly, describing her as a gentle, loving, simple, yet shrewd Scottish matron, such as Sir Walter Scott has taught us to venerate.

Nor must the fact be omitted that she stood on Sir Walter's list of friends, and was one of his recognised favourites. He always made his way to her in Edinburgh society, if she happened to be present, and nothing could draw him from her side when she opened her "auld world" stories, of which she had no end. The charm may have been the greater from the link of connexion with his own associations, which carried him back to the Regent Morton and the Lady of Lochlevin, whom she lineally represented. "She was a true Helen Douglas," we learn from her nephew, and her worth receives further testimony in his own character, which she helped to form, and so inspired with the chivalrous spirit of his race.

And it may have been from her that he derived some of his minor traits, his playful humour, his happy art in storytelling, and his love of music and flowers. The only drawback to Mrs. Baillie's lessons seems to have been the pure Doric in which they were imparted, so clearly marking her nationality that it could not be disguised by her best English. Of this she had proof on one occasion, when she entered a confectioner's shop in London, and addressed herself to the man at the counter, inquiring, "Have you got any sweetmeats for the children?"

"Oh, ay, a' got sweeties for the bairns," was the reply, in a somewhat resentful tone.

"I did not say sweeties for the bairns," rejoined Mrs. Baillie.

"Ay, but ye *suld* have said it," retorted the confectioner, who it is needless to say came from the right side of the Tweed.

Little Howard repaid the love of his aunt with a tender affection which sprang up at once and never declined. An incident of his childhood evinces the existence both of this attachment and of the manliness that marked his character even at that time.

One day his aunt received a visit from a lady who had not seen him before, and she asked Mrs. Baillie who he was, and why he was staying at Musselburg, when he ran forward and answered for himself. "My name is Howard Douglas: my mamma is dead, my papa's at sea, and that's why I am here with my own dear auntie." No one could have better told his history, and his words and air so charmed the lady that she regarded him afterwards with maternal interest.

Much might have been learnt of this period of his life from the correspondence of Mrs. Baillie with her brother, but unfortunately only three of her letters can be found, and but one makes reference to the children in her charge. This was written on the 1st of January, 1782, and Sir Charles sailed from Plymouth on the 2nd, so that it may not have reached his hands till after the great battle of the 12th of April.

I received yours of the 18th *ultimo*, from Plymouth, Saturday last. Well do you conceive my anxiety about you at present. Our lovely three (his children) have been to us all this day—all happy and well. Gracious God, grant that their father and protector may be soon and happily restored to them and me again. How happy should I be to see that your only employment was attending to the rearing and educating of those sweet sensible lambs. . . . Says Howard, 'I will pray for papa,' and miss in this, as in everything else, 'So will I too.' . . . .

Mr. Baillie's best compliments of the season, and prays that you may be successful in humbling the pride of the enemies of Great Britain. I send best wishes to my dear William (his eldest son, who accompanied him to sea).

Remember, my dear Charles, that Lieutenant Congelton of the *Yarmouth* is cousin to our own beloved now angel mother. Let him know that I have wrote to you about him. Praying for your health and preservation,

> I remain, in haste, my dear Charles,
>> Your very indebted and attached sister,
>>> Helena Baillie.

The tidings of the victory reached Musselburg in the autumn, and were read aloud by Mrs. Baillie to the children, making such an impression on little Howard that he never forgot the scene. From this moment all his aspirations were inspired by the exploits of his father and the thought of himself becoming a sailor. Though not yet emancipated from his nursery governess, he found a never-failing attraction in a pond in the garden, where he could launch and manoeuvre his toy ships, which received constant additions from Mrs. Baillie, who knew that his father destined him for the sea, and so encouraged his nautical tastes.

Sir Charles paid a visit to his sister during a stay on shore, and was entreated by Howard to go to the pond and review his fleet. He playfully consented, expecting a child's show, and was surprised to find the little vessels set in squadrons with professional skill. The display touched a chord near his heart, and he broke into an exclamation of pleasure, as he recognised his boy as a born tar.

Howard ascended from the governess to a tutor, and subsequently entered the grammar-school, but his chief study was still the same, and he spent every leisure hour on the lake at Fisher Row, where he formed intimacies with fisher-lads, and afterwards with youths be-longing to the vessels that frequented the port. Hence, he became so initiated in seamanship that he could manage a fishing-boat or a ship's yawl, and often made his escape to sea in one of these craft, to the great alarm of his aunt and *dominie*.

But an event shortly happened that changed the course of his life, disappointing the aspirations he had formed, and placing him in a new position. In the spring of 1789 Sir Charles Douglas was appointed commander-in-chief on a foreign station and hoisted his flag at Ports-mouth, when he paid a hasty visit to Scotland, to bring away Howard, and take him on board his own ship to sea. He arrived at Musselburg in the midst of the excitement caused by the recovery of George III. from his first illness, and intended to take part in the rejoicings, but a -sudden attack of illness confined him to his room. This was not al-lowed to interfere with the enjoyment of his children, and they went to a juvenile ball at a neighbour's, given in honour of the occasion.

It is indicative of the thoughtful kindness inherent in Howard that he ran over from the dance to see his father several times during the evening. He found him complaining of pain in the head, and saw that he was disturbed by the glare of the illumination, which he proposed to shut out by darkening the window. "God forbid that my window should be the first darkened on such a night as this!" said the old ad-miral, showing his ruling passion of loyalty strong in death: for these were his last words. He was seized with apoplexy during the night, and the morning found him dead.

CHAPTER 2

Young Days

The destiny of Howard Douglas was now in the hands of his guardians, and they judged it inexpedient to carry out his father's design of placing him in the navy, considering that he might interfere with the prospects of his two half-brothers, who were already in the service. Hence, they applied to have him nominated for admission into the Royal Academy at Woolwich, without deeming it necessary to consult himself; and he first heard of their plans on being ordered to proceed to Woolwich for examination, in the summer of 1790. He thus began life with the surrender of his ambition; and his sense of disappointment must have been bitter indeed, for he spoke of it to the last. But he yielded without a murmur: it was his first lesson in duty, and he was to prove that duty weighed with him above every other feeling.

There is nothing to show whether his attainments underwent polishing before he left Musselburg as a preparation for the approaching examination; but a voyage to London in a Scotch smack was too fruitful of interest to a spoiled sailor not to efface such instruction if received. He was now actually in a ship at sea, and could help to haul the ropes, and even mount the rigging, while he charmed the sailors by his familiarity with the tackle, and the sublimest nautical phrases. In fact, he spent those happy days in learning navigation instead of poring over Euclid, and arrived at Woolwich in first-rate order for the midshipman's berth, but not so qualified for the academy.

Time had been when the gate of the establishment stood wide, and admission was an easy affair. But in 1773 the Inspector of Instruction came in contact with a young gentleman unacquainted with the alphabet; and it was thought prudent to insist that every candidate should "not only understand reading and writing," (Records of the Royal Military Academy), but even the Rule of Three. From this simple beginning the standard of qualification had advanced until it embraced a certain proficiency in mathematics, and Howard Douglas went up on this test, and was plucked.

The anguish of that moment he never forgot. He turned away from the examiners with drooping head and a look of despair, conscious only of rejection. But the power which the song declares to sit up aloft watched over the little sailor. Though turned back, he had displayed the ability opening in his mind; and the mathematical professor told him he was sure to do, and bade him take courage and try again. It had flashed across him that he might avoid the humiliation of returning disgraced to his friends by running to sea, changing his name, and leaving no clue by which he might be traced. But those kind words brought him to a clearer perception of his duty, and a belief in his power to succeed. The courage they told him to cherish he had never lost; and the ungraded boy of thirteen now walked through Woolwich looking for a competent teacher.

His little stock of money forbade his applying to the expensive grinders of the town; but it would seem that he already possessed the germ of that insight into character which marked his maturer years, and he found a skilled mathematician in the master of an obscure day-school, whose abilities he was the first to discover. Within three weeks he again presented himself at the academy, and passed the examination in triumph. Six weeks more found him at the head of the mathematical class; and he attained such proficiency, that Dr. Hutton always told any boy in a difficulty to "go to Douglas." The pupil reciprocated the appreciation of his master, and ever spoke of him with gratitude; nor can there be a doubt that he remembered him to the last; for his biographer found a medallion of Dr. Hutton in the box containing his latest papers.

The cadets of those days were left great liberty in their movements, though regulations existed for maintaining discipline, and attempts were continually made at improvement. It had been found necessary to ordain that no one should "presume to go out after tattoo, either *over* the wall or any other way;" but there would seem to have been no other way, as the porter locked the gates at tattoo. Another injunction forbade any cadet to carve his name on the desks, or to break open the desks or drawers of the inspectors, professors, and masters; and the regulations went so far as to add—"or even to attempt to take anything out of them under the name of smouching;" though the prefatory "even" seemed to admit this was rather arbitrary.

The cadets were cautioned against employing school-hours in

reading light works under cover of studying their tasks; and also, against throwing, stones at the masters, which the regulations declared a capital offence, though they thought it capital fun. The masters themselves came in for admonition; and a manifesto from the lieutenant-governor complains that the cadets:

> Are frequently left without either professor or master for the space of half an hour, and sometimes for much longer time, by which neglect they remain totally unoccupied in any study, and are besides, by the absence of the controlling power, led into very disorderly and improper behaviour. (Records of the Royal Military Academy, Woolwich, 1861.)

The cadets' barrack stood in the Warren, on a spot since occupied by the buildings of the Royal Arsenal; and Colonel Wilmot has engraved a representation of it as it appeared about 1790. This shows a row of trees in the front, overshadowing a lawn, where a couple of cadets are seen reclining, while they receive the greetings of a third, got up as the *beau* of the company. He wears a scarlet coat, frilled shirt, and top-boots, arranged to expose striped silk stockings, and has given his arm to another character of the time, a lackadaisical-looking youth, known as the "ladies' man." This group pays no heed to a knot of cadets at the barrack door, standing by a four-horse coach, on which the attendants are stowing their luggage, and which is to carry them home for the summer holidays. Two others are settling accounts with Mother Montagu, the cake-woman; and a third is seen at a window above, waiting to efface his score in another way, by sluicing her with water.

Such was the little world in which Howard Douglas suddenly found himself a notable. Having been only six weeks in the academy, he must have become chief of his class while he was a *neux*, the title borne by the junior of a room. As such, he was expected to discharge those offices which could not be imposed on the small complement of servants; such as bringing in the water to wash for dinner, making the tea, and toasting the bread. Indeed, custom bound him to obey every command of the head of the room, though the *neux* is never required to do anything degrading, like the fags of other schools; and it is certain that Howard's yoke was not heavy, as he never made it a subject of complaint.

Nor would many have thus ventured to put him on his mettle, for his bold and fearless nature made itself felt in a manner that precluded oppression; and he was soon as much a leader in the playground as the schoolroom. If he ever knew fear, he took every occasion to show that he held it in contempt; for none of the cadets approached him in feats of daring. One of his gambols was to run close to the line of fire when the company was exercised with artillery, and this gained him something more than schoolboy plaudits, though only done in bravado, for his alert eye caught points in the practice which he afterwards turned to account. Sir Hew Ross describes him as more prudent during the latter part of his stay at the academy, as he would then have been the first to prevent any one running into danger, and he had acquired such influence in the company that few would pursue what he opposed.

The vicinity of the Thames afforded him opportunities of nautical practice, which he did not neglect, though they could only be pursued under restrictions; for the authorities of the academy kept a jealous eye on the river, and the regulations ordained that "the first cadet that is found swimming in the Thames shall be taken out naked and put in the guard-room." But he managed to be enough on the water to keep in his hand, and he always spread a sail in blowing weather, which brought out his points, while he paid more than one visit to Deptford Dockyard in search of higher knowledge.

The holidays secured him a larger experience, for then he had the range of the Berwick and Leith smacks, in which he took his passage to and from Scotland, where he spent the interval. On board these craft he learned the mysteries of knotting and splicing, of plaiting points and gaskets, and of making grammets, and became expert in heaving the lead. We hear nothing from him of his reputation at the academy at this period, and the good opinions he won from all around; but a memorandum of the time betrays his predilections by referring to his sailorcraft. He notes:

I will venture to say, I know as much of cutter-sailing as any middy or mate in His Majesty's Navy.

His enthusiasm for the sea had been sustained by the reverence he cherished for his father, which was of the deepest kind; for he observed the anniversary of his death as a sacred day through a period of seventy-two years. A packet among his papers attracted his biographer by a label in his own hand which revealed this veneration in the inscription—

Relating to the services of my honoured father.

The old name was now to be signalised by his own services in a career as brilliant.

CHAPTER 3

In Commission

The events passing at this time occupied every mind. The heart thrills at the incidents of the French Revolution even in the present day, and how must they have been felt when the Reign of Terror was in progress, and society looked on! It constantly seemed that human wickedness had reached its limit, when the newspapers reported atrocities which out-horrored what had gone before. War heightened the excitement, and strained every nerve of England, obliging her to maintain the forces of her allies as well as her own, and guard all her possessions, while she stood in fear for her own soil.

The English people fired at this danger, and all classes caught the fervour. The most enterprising flocked to the army or navy; the agricultural population recruited the militia; the towns swarmed with volunteers; and the combined services numbered as many as 800,000 men at one period of the struggle. The island might then have been likened to a fortress, and the nation to its garrison.

Young Douglas felt all the influence of such surroundings. He had begun to note public events in his childhood, when his perceptions were quickened by the exploits of his father in the war with the American colonies, and this gave him a political bias even at that time. The impression deepened as he grew up, and stood a witness of the French Revolution, and the ruin it spread through Europe. His patriotism was inborn, but it expanded under the pressure of the time, till the danger of invasion made love of country his dominant feeling.

Thus his life was a testimony of devotion to England, showing him ever zealous to promote her greatness, and shield her from misfortune; nor can the most factious complain that he sought these ejects by a Conservative course, since he had seen the country reel before the popular movements of his youth, one of which stripped her of half her dominions, wide the other imperilled her existence.

The same faith animated his old age, after an experience of eighty years, and was reflected in devotion to the State, loyalty to the Crown, and a deep sense of religion. The vulgar notion of a Tory found no warrant in such a character, who withstood innovation, but advocated progress, and always invited discussion. It might be well if vaunted Liberals would allow the same freedom, and show the same respect for opponents. One who knew him well (the chaplain-general, in a letter to the author), writes:

> I never heard him speak ill, or even unkindly, of anyone. If he disapproved of the conduct or opinions of others, he would say so; but always with apparent regret. His mind was too full of higher things to have space for envy or bitterness.

Sir Hew Ross mentions that he bore the same character in 1795, when he received his first commission, and left the academy for the Royal Artillery. He was now seventeen, and might be satisfied with the position he had attained, though not in the profession he would have chosen. He had stepped in advance of older lads, competing for the same prize, which was awaited with such impatience that some were even tempted to don the artillery uniform before their appointment. (Records of the Royal Military Academy.) The uniform is still a fascination, and exercises such a spell over newly-appointed officers that they are said to sleep in it the first week.

Exclusion from the vocation of our choice is often made an excuse for failure, but the power of election is given to few, and industry will make way in any pursuit, however uncongenial. Lieutenant Douglas indulged in no regrets over lost prospects, but threw himself into the profession he had adopted, though his preference for the navy remained unchanged, and though he seized every opportunity of mixing with sailors. Nor was he satisfied with discharging only such duties as he could not avoid. He took his profession in hand, and sought to extend its bounds, so mastering the incidence of artillery that he could seize any opening for bringing it into play. He wished to be a good officer, and hence perfected himself in drill and manoeuvring, and qualified himself to act in any capacity, by observing and sketching country, and practising reconnaissance. His turn for mechanics attracted him to the workshop, but he did not neglect the laboratory, and took care to keep up his proficiency in mathematics.

His merit was recognised immediately, and he had been in the corps but a few months when he was despatched to Tynemouth Castle, to take command of the artillery in the northern district. The expulsion of the Duke of York from Holland had increased the danger of invasion, since it left that country to the enemy, whose armies were thus placed on our flank as well as our front, while they possessed a port of aggression in Antwerp. Yet parts of our coasts were left unprotected, and Lieutenant Douglas found such a gap in his command in the north. The detachment consisted of only two sergeants, four corporals, and thirty gunners at Tynemouth; a non-commissioned officer and three gunners at Sunderland; the same number at Hartlepool; and a small body of invalid artillery at Berwick.

The day after his arrival he represented the insufficiency of the force to General Nesbit Balfour, the officer in command of the district, and the general forwarded his report to the higher authorities, backing it with a demand for reinforcement. But he asked for what did not exist, and learnt that he must make the most of his numbers, as they could receive no addition. The answer brought the general to the end of his devices. He saw the artillerymen at Tynemouth were too few to man the guns, but he had made the fact known in the proper quarter, and there was nothing more to be done.

Lieutenant Douglas suggested that they might find a resource. He proposed that a detachment of thirty men should be sent to Tynemouth Castle from every regiment in the district, together with a subaltern, and that he should train them in the service of two field-guns, which would enable them to act as artillery.

The scheme was approved by the general, who ordered down two detachments at once, and these were succeeded by others, till the required number were trained. But the young officer required something more, and success urged him to further effort. He could only be satisfied with efficiency, and he was still without force to man sixty heavy guns in battery at the fort intended to rake the mouth of the Tyne. His intercourse with the town assured him of the patriotic spirit of the merchants and shipowners, and he suggested to the general to call them together, and recommend the formation of a corps of gunners from the men in their employment.

General Balfour seems to have had a faculty for appreciating his conceptions, though they came from a subordinate, and the project was set on foot. It met a warm response, bringing to his aid five hundred young men, whom he enrolled in companies, and trained in the service of the guns—first with blank cartridge, and afterwards with shot at floating targets. (*The Defence of England*, by General Sir Howard Douglas.) Thus, he placed Tynemouth in a good posture of defence.

Such occupation left him little leisure, but he found time to indulge his passion for sailoring, and made himself master of a sea-boat which he delighted to take out in squally weather. It was his practice to board vessels trading to the port, and accompany them into harbour, whence he contracted friendships with the captains and mates, and obtained from them valuable instruction. Sometimes he took a party of friends for a sail, and remained afloat for the day, when he regaled them with sailor's fare a little improved.

One summer morning he was cruising about with a brother-officer, when they espied two young ladies of their acquaintance sufficiently near to claim recognition. Lieutenant Douglas thought he could do nothing less than run the boat in, and invite them to a sail round the harbour, and his companion took the same view. The invitation was kindly received, though the ladies felt obliged to decline from motives of propriety: but they could not resist a little chat, and this drew them nearer the boat, in which two captivating lieutenants were waiting to renew the temptation. It then met a fainter refusal, and one young lady thought there could be no harm in going halfway across the harbour, to which the other was persuaded to accede.

But this tied young ladies and captivating lieutenants to impossible conditions. Who could remember such a compact when the breeze on the water was so refreshing, the morning so fine, the company so good, and the conversation so engrossing? Instead of turning back in the middle of the harbour, the boat stood out to sea; wine and eatables were produced, and it was not till the day wore on that the fair cruisers remembered the account they must render on their return home.

They then became alarmed, and the two officers pushed for the shore, anxious to cover their trespass. For some days they were impatient to learn the issue; but the ladies did not appear at their usual resorts, and they remained in a state of uncertainty. Three weeks elapsed, and it is to be feared that they had forgotten both the occurrence and the young ladies, when the younger one was seen by Lieutenant Douglas at an attic-window, looking inconsolable—Patience on a monument, without her smile. Afterwards they met at a ball, and it transpired that both ladies had been kept prisoners, and now were only at large under guard.

The North was full of uniforms—regulars, militia, and volunteers—so that there was no end of revelry and good fellowship. One of the militia regiments had for its colonel the Duke of Norfolk, who fitted up his quarters as a wine-cellar, and there gave sumptuous entertainments. But few quarters at Tynemouth could be adapted to such uses, as the town was so packed with military, that officers could only be stowed in holes and corners. Lieutenant Douglas occupied a room barely habitable, and had to contest the tenancy with rats, which asserted their claim with such tenacity, that he went to sleep at the risk of being devoured.

Their incursions compelled him to furnish himself with loaded pistols and a tinder-box, and he kept watch one night, remaining quiet till there was an irruption, when he started up and struck a light. But his vigilance proved of no avail, for the clink of the flint and steel caused a stampede, and not a rat remained by the time he had kindled the tinder. Their flight suggested to him another device. He looked out all the holes, and covered them with slides, connected with each other by wires, and these he fastened to a string, which enabled him to draw them all with one pull, and thus close the outlets.

The contrivance claims to be mentioned as his first success in mechanics, foreshadowing his future expertness. It came into use the same night: he pulled the string without rising from bed, then struck a light, while the rats flew off to the holes to find them blocked, and he shot them at leisure. Two or three such massacres cleared off the intruders, and left him undisturbed in his quarters.

CHAPTER 4

Adventures at Sea

Early in August, 1795, Lieutenant Douglas was ordered to take charge of a detachment of troops with women and children, and proceed to Quebec in the *Phillis* transport. He joined the ship at Gravesend, and found himself the senior officer on board, in command of six subalterns. But he was not so elated by his position as by the prospect of a voyage across the Atlantic, which afforded scope for the exercise of his seamanship, and whatever time could be spared from his duties was given to this object.

There is an impression of awe in our first experience of the ocean, when we lose sight of the shore which enchains us by so many ties, and from which we cannot part without a pang, even in boyhood. Who can say we shall ever rejoin the friends we leave behind, or at what time we shall return, if ever? Change and uncertainty are suggested by every object—by the rolling ship, the toppling waves, the vast expanse bounded by clouds, and the sky hanging from immensity. They strike the mind of youth like an allegory, stirring thought to its depths, and one moment imparts a burst of character that might else be the work of years. It cannot be known that such an inspiration swayed Lieutenant Douglas; but the voyage showed this development in his faculties, and gave the lad of nineteen a lead among men.

We now describe the Atlantic passage as a trip; but it was a serious undertaking in those days, when the fastest ships were heavy sailers, and comfort at sea unknown. The *Phillis* went her own pace, and week after week advanced her but little on the voyage, though Lieutenant Douglas saw no ground for complaint, for they were favoured with very bad weather, and this afforded fine opportunities of turning out at night and going aloft in a gale of wind. None of the crew excelled him in reefing, and he often appeared at the weather-earring, and sometimes at the lee, in heavy lurches. Such a pleasure could not be enjoyed at ease for any length of time; and the pinch came in an appreciable shape, when the steward announced the failure of the fresh provisions.

Nothing could be made of salt pork and biscuit in a musty state, and there was slender prospect of improvement; for the vessel had been nine weeks out before they sighted the island of St. Peter's, about forty leagues to the east of. the southern entrance of the Gulf of St. Lawrence. Here they met a tempest which placed them in great danger, a mountainous wave striking the ship, and tearing both her boats from their lashings. The boats were thrown on the deck and with difficulty secured, as the sea had swept off their chocks, and they could only be lashed bottom upwards. This caused little concern at the time, but proved of consequence when their services were required.

The gale subsided next day, and then fell to a calm, which was succeeded by a light breeze. There seemed a promise of better weather, and this brought up the women and children, who had rarely been able to appear on deck, and now enjoyed the fresh air. But danger arose in the midst of congratulation, and again drove them below. The military officers were spending the evening in the cabin, and the captain had joined the party, when he was called out by the mate, and they hastened on deck together. Something in their manner alarmed Lieutenant Douglas, and he followed them unobserved, reaching the deck at the same moment. He had no need to inquire their situation; for his ear caught the roar of breakers, and their proximity was attested by the sound, though they could not be seen in the darkness.

The clouds overhead seemed to meet the waves, as they rose up at the side—a wall of water, and the yard-arm almost dipped, as the gale burst in gusts through the rigging, heeling the vessel on her beam. The scene appalled the crew, of whom only two were English, and they stood helpless, though their lives depended on action. The captain applied to Lieutenant Douglas for the assistance of the soldiers, who were turned up, and all hands set to bend the cables and let go the best bower-anchor. It fell in about twenty-five fathoms water, and seemed to check the ship, though a strong current was running towards the breakers, and nautical eyes discovered land on both quarters like a bank of cloud, bringing the dreadful conviction that they were embayed.

Wreck was even nearer than it appeared, for they presently found there was no hold in the anchor, and nothing remained but to take to the boats. But it was first necessary to weather a reef on the lee bow, which could only be accomplished by making more sail, and the crew were ordered aloft to shake out a reef. To attempt such a task seemed death, when the gale broke in thunder-claps, the darkness hid the spars, the masts bent like twigs, and the ship floundered in foam. The sailors shrank back, and none would obey the order. Their defection confounded the captain, but he knew there were brave men in the ship, and called for volunteers.

One sprang into the shrouds on the instant, it was Lieutenant Douglas; and his example drew out the two cabin-boys, who were English, and followed him aloft, one helping to shake out a reef of the close-reefed main-topsail, while the other loosed the main-topgallant-sail. The next few moments were passed in an agony of suspense. The ship laboured as for life, plunging and rocking, her canvas strained to splitting, and bearing her nearer and nearer the reef, which was marked by the raging breakers, riveting the gaze of men, women, and children. Happily, she cleared the point; for otherwise all must have perished, as it shut off the land, and left them no approach.

Lieutenant Douglas now rushed below to secure his valuables, but had mislaid the key of his desk. There was no time for a search, and he broke it open, taking out his father's watch, the only thing he saved, and fastening it in his belt. He threw off his redundant clothes, to be prepared for swimming—which proved a happy thought—and then caught up a child from the waist, and flew back to the deck. He was attended by a faithful companion, a Newfoundland dog, which followed him wherever he went, though never impeding his movements. But the child was past rescue, and only clung to his breast an instant, when it died without a moan.

He found the sailors bringing up some fowling-pieces and powder, with a quantity of clothes and provisions, and stowing them in the boats, which were fitted with yard and stay tackle, and hoisted away. But the manner in which they had been secured on drifting made them unhandy, and a surge of the sea caught the bottom of the long-boat as it swung in the weather roll, and dashed it to pieces. The next wave grappled the ship, shook her from stem to stern, and flung her on a sunken rock.

The terror of the crash was heightened by the conduct of the crew, who lost all self-control, "behaving like cowards," (copy of letter from Lieutenant Douglas to Captain Frazer, in the *Douglas Papers*), and by the frantic cries of the women and children, the roar of the storm and the sea, the quivering of the ship, and the spectacle of the foaming waters, almost lighting up the darkness. Lieutenant Douglas writes, (*Douglas Papers*):

> That horrible scene, baffles all description, nor can the most lively imagination conceive half its horrors.

Again and again the ship struck the rock, each time with the same violence and the same terribly effect. But, she still drifted towards the shore, and this was not more than a quarter of a mile distant; so, there were hopes that it might be reached in the remaining boat. It had hitherto been in shadow, but the moon now appeared, and showed a black iron coast, rising perpendicularly from the breakers. There could be no doubt that it was uninhabited, and every heart quailed at its bare wild aspect, hardly less frightful than the gulf between.

The captain called on the crew to man the tackle and lower the boat, but only the two mates and the carpenter responded. These were joined by Lieutenant Douglas and two of his comrades, Lieutenants Caddy and Forbes (later General Forbes, Colonel Commandant of the Royal Artillery), but their united efforts could hardly get the boat over the side. It then seemed that she would stave the ship, and Douglas jumped in to keep her off, followed by Forbes and Caddy. But the boat was already half full of water, and they were obliged to spring back, in doing which Douglas missed his footing and fell into the sea.

The boat dashed against the ship the same moment, breaking in pieces, but he kept afloat by swimming till a wave lifted him up and Forbes seized his collar and dragged him on deck. This did not place him in safety, for the vessel was found to be sinking and everyone expected instant destruction. A few awaited their fate with composure, some broke into a frenzy of terror, others threw themselves on their knees in prayer, and those who could swim stripped themselves for a last struggle with the waves. But the ship drifted on for a quarter of an hour and then settled on the slope of a bank, which kept her deck above water, and it became possible that she might hold together till daylight. The letter of Lieutenant Douglas says:

> We stood during the remainder of that long, long night, wet through with the continual dashing of the breakers, eagerly wishing for day.

And day took away their last hope—the hope that had buoyed them through the night; for it showed them the impossibility of reaching the shore without assistance, the space between being studded with rocks, through which the high waves surged in floods, forming a cauldron of foam; and they saw themselves cut off from escape within fifteen yards of the land. The situation nerved one of the crew with the courage of despair, and he suddenly jumped overboard and struck boldly out, rising on a high sea and wrestling with the waves. He disappeared in the surging foam, but rose again, lifted himself over the breakers, and gained the beach. Here he was caught by a rushing surf, which dashed him against the rocks, and he was seen no more.

His progress had been watched from the ship as if every life depended on his—with strained eyes and bated breath. They were so absorbed by the sight that they heeded neither the drenching spray from above nor the quivering of the ship under their feet, and they burst into a cry as they saw him perish. But he had gained the beach before he was swamped, and this brought forward one of the artillery officers, who undertook to make fast a hawser to the shore, and thus rescue all.

The name of this brave lad was Barclay, and his good nature had won the esteem of everyone on board; but he could not be dissuaded from the step he proposed, though eyes filled with tears as he threw off his clothes. He took an affecting leave of his brother officers, gave one look round, and plunged into the sea. They watched for his reappearance, but only to see him throw up his arms and sink for ever.

The horror of the incident was scarcely felt in the danger of the moment, for a mountainous wave struck the ship, and threatened all with the same fate. Lieutenant Barnes was washed out of the forechains, where he had posted himself to watch Barclay, and engulfed in the sea. Another wave broke over the deck and tore Mrs. D'Ellmonville from the arms of her husband, sweeping her overboard in the same way, and a soldier's wife was seen holding her two children above the wave till they sunk together. Sea upon sea struck the ship, and successive breaches carried off half a dozen others, Lieutenant Barclay's servant following his master and bearing with him one of the boys who had accompanied Lieutenant Douglas aloft.

All were drenched to the skin and almost frozen with exposure, while they had now been many hours without food, but the motion prevented them going below for supplies, and they famished with abundance at hand. In this extremity the mate secured a piece of raw pork and a cheese which he saw floating in the scuppers, and these were cut up and distributed amongst the company, everyone receiving a share. It formed the only meal of the day, and again night closed around, while the storm raged unabated.

The prospect of another night on the wreck appalled the bravest, and the women became stupefied with terror, crouching over their children, whose cries they could not still. The wind howled through the rigging; the sea washed the deck, or burst against the bulwarks, throwing over torrents of spray; the masts threatened to snap or go by the board; and the roar of the breakers was deafening. The after part of the ship began to settle, and every lurch shook the cabin bell, which rang dismally, and blended with the whine of Douglas's dog, seeming to knell their doom. A sailor made a push at the dog, and shoved it overboard to see if it would reach the shore; and soon it was heard from the nearest point, where it remained all night whining and howling. Such were the sights and sounds for hour on hour.

The women lost their hold of the ropes and were washed overboard, with one exception: nor did the strongest men expect to see morning. Four of the crew determined to seek refuge below, and contrived to descend the main hatchway, where they obtained a light, and broke into the store-room. Here they found a cask of rum, and their draughts were deep and long, till they became mad drunk; and the gale brought up their shouts of laughter, mingled with curses and snatches of song. It was like the revelry of demons, exulting in the darkness and tempest, and heightening their horrors. But these orgies hushed as the night advanced; nothing was heard but the raging of the storm, and the hatchway gave out the silence of death. The drunkards had sunk into sleep, and two of them never awoke.

The weather moderated towards morning, and it became possible to move about the deck, which suggested immediate action; and Lieutenant Douglas proposed the construction of a raft capable of bearing two or three men, who might aid the rescue of the rest. His counsel was adopted, and two of the crew succeeded in landing. But they wandered off inland, without carrying out their orders, and regardless of shouts from the wreck and the captain's signals, which they showed no intention of obeying. Their desertion caused the more dismay, as the wreck was found to be sinking, and the chance of escape lessened with every moment. Not a heart but throbbed while the carpenter prepared another raft; no one ventured to speak; and the ear thrilled with the ring of the hammers and clatter of spars.

Then came the splash of the launch; it floated and lived; and the second mate, carpenter, and two seamen pushed for the shore. There they established a bridge to the wreck by making fast a hawser from the bowsprit, and all on board were brought safe to land.

CHAPTER 5

Cast Away

They had hardly assembled on the cliff when the wreck began to part, and the channel between became strewn with broken plank and drifts from the cargo. But there was nothing around to make their escape seem fortunate. The country imaged desolation, rising from the sea in masses of rock capped with snow, and spreading back in rugged tracts seamed with hollows and gullies. On every side rose mountains clothed with forests, which looked impenetrable, and had never been entered by man, while not a trace appeared of bird or beast. The snow lay deep on the ground, and the blast swept up from the sea, driving them for shelter to a thicket of spruce-trees, where it was decided to pass the night. Fortunately, some bales of cloth were washed ashore, and these were torn in pieces and equally distributed, supplying everyone with a wrapper.

Thus, the day closed, and the shivering company huddled together, quailing under the gathering clouds, which grew blacker and blacker; and night had hardly begun when rain fell in floods. Yet the two nights on the wreck had caused such exhaustion that it prevailed over wet and cold, and all fell asleep. A frost set in, and they must have been frozen to death, only that Lieutenant Douglas was aroused by a scream. This broke from his servant's wife, who had been brought ashore insensible—the only woman who survived—and now started from a disturbed sleep. He awoke her husband and gave her into his charge, while he dragged himself through the party and made them all get up, his own paralysed limbs assuring him that they would perish otherwise. They were all stiffening, and ascribed their preservation to his forethought, though they lay down again after stirring a little, being quite worn out.

But they were now kept awake by the cries of the suffering woman, to whom the scene had given another shock, and she started up mad. Her husband and his master drew her back and held her down, while they tried to soothe; but persuasion fell void on her ear, and she raved and shrieked for hours. Her voice blended with the rain and wind—now in wail, now with a piercing cry, a torrent of fierce words, or exclamations of despair. But nature snapped under the strain; the voice spoke no longer; and the storm resounded alone: the last woman was dead.

Lieutenant Douglas seemed to have but closed his eyes after this horror when he was awakened by day, which cleared away the clouds, and brought warmth and sunshine. He mentions that "the sun shone forth with great power—the greatest blessing the Almighty could send us." (Letter to Captain Frazer.) It enabled them to dry their tinder, soaked through on its way ashore, and they kindled a fire, the drifts from the wreck supplying fuel. The cold and rain had caused great suffering during the night, rendering several helpless, and Lieutenant Bennett and Ensign Truscott were found insensible. They were brought to the fire and their limbs warmed by rubbing, when Douglas moistened their lips with wine, a cask having broken from the wreck and washed ashore. They rallied after a time, but remained, powerless, and their limbs proved to be frost-bitten. Wine was needed by others, but the crew seized the cask and carried it to the cliff, where they shared the contents, and were soon rolling about drunk, or fighting over the dregs.

Lieutenant Douglas preserved his authority over the soldiers, and they behaved well, with two exceptions, remaining together, and obeying his orders. He employed them in collecting the drift from the wreck, and thus secured the broken timber, and a quantity of smoked pork which had formed the cargo, so that they had now no lack of supplies, and the whole company gathered round the fire and made a common meal. They afterwards deliberated as to the course they should follow, and Douglas pronounced for remaining on the spot, and erecting a beacon, which they might expect to attract the notice of any passing ship.

But it was objected that no vessel was likely to come within sight there, the shore being out of the track of navigation, and known as dangerous; nor would they have approached it themselves but for their run before the tempest. Hence, they could only be delivered by making their way to a settlement, and one could hardly fail to be reached if they penetrated to the interior. Such reasoning convinced nearly all, but it was agreed to wait two days for Truscott and Bennett, as Douglas protested against their being abandoned, though he admitted that everyone must depend on his own exertions.

Little hope could be entertained that the two officers would recover; but they sank so rapidly that the time granted seemed the verge of their lives. He remained with them till the last moment, when both were delirious, while their pulse was scarcely perceptible, and their feet were like stone. Assured they were beyond help, he joined the party on the cliff, and they moved away through the frozen rain and snow, each man wrapped in his cloak, and bearing as much provision as he could carry. He writes, (to Captain Frazer):

> In solemn silence, we continued our day's journey over almost inaccessible mountains and through almost impenetrable woods, till about two o'clock, when we took up our quarters for the night in a wood on the side of a hill.

Here they made a fire; water was procured from a stream in the forest, and everyone received a ration of pork. But food and rest came too late for two of the party, who sank from fatigue, and the survivors laid their bodies outside the wood, as they had no means of digging a grave. In vain they sought to forget their misery in sleep; for those who yielded to drowsiness awoke benumbed, and passed the remainder of the night in suffering. But this did not prevent them limping off with the others at sunrise, for to remain behind was death. And the sun now gave no warmth, but gleamed through clouds heavy with rain, while they dragged their way through the snow in the teeth of a cutting wind.

A man dropped from the ranks, then a second, and a third, perishing where they fell, and the hardiest began to admit the obstacles to success. Nor had they power to go further; for they stood in a valley blocked with trees and walled in by mountains, which poured down swollen torrents, forming an impassable river in their front. The prospect brought all to a stand, and it was agreed to abandon the enterprise, and return to the bay.

Imagination could add nothing to the long agony of their march back, which broke down some of the strongest; but youth and vigour sustained Lieutenant Douglas, and he led the party in. Only one thought possessed his mind on reaching the cliffs— a thought so absorbing that it raised a hope, and he dragged himself into the wood in search of Truscott and Bennett. He was so spent that he could hardly proceed, though he now saw their bodies stretched on the ground on the spot where they were left. But he hardly believed his eyes as he advanced; for the sound of his steps spread through the thicket, and the two officers looked round—they were alive!

It appeared that they had regained consciousness almost at the same time, and cheered each other in their misery, sustaining themselves with the food placed within reach. Their looks presented sad evidence of suffering; but they had youth on their side, and their tenacity of life induced hopes that they might recover, procuring them every attention that circumstances permitted, as the company straggled to the spot, marvelling to find them alive. The weariness of the scene was broken by a fire kindled by the soldiers, and round this they all grouped, remaining quiet for the night, and obtaining what rest they could.

The next morning, they exerted themselves to carry put the plan of Lieutenant Douglas, erecting a beacon on the cliffs, formed of the mainmast of the ship; and this they furnished with a flag of black cloth stitched to a piece of canvas, an object visible at a great distance. Others were employed in building a hut, for which he cleared a space in the middle of the thicket, sparing such trees as were in a right line as supports for the sides. These consisted of planks from the wreck raised to a height of three feet and a half, and bound to the trees by lashings, strengthened outside by stakes in the ground.

The side most exposed to the sea received a further defence in a wall of stones raised to the same height, and faced with a thick coat of sods to keep out the wind and spray. Rafters were laid above, supporting the roof, which was formed of planks, also covered in with sods, but with a small hole in the centre for a chimney. They had nearly completed the hut by night, and next day gave them a refuge which would not have been scorned by Robinson Crusoe.

But this afforded little defence against the climate; and they saw another terror in their slender stock of provisions, which would not long supply their dole of food. Mutiny added a new element to their misery. The sailors found some casks of wine and a quantity of pork and cheeses, which had drifted to the beach at some distance, and refused to give them up, carrying them to another thicket, where they formed a bivouac of their own. The wine attracted a few of the soldiers, and they were leaving the hut for the wood when Lieutenant Douglas called them back.

"No more of your orders," answered their ringleader, defiantly.

"We're all equal now."

Douglas flew at his throat with a knife. "We are equals in misfortune," he said, "and your officers are willing to bear equally all your privations; but you shall discharge your duty, and we will be obeyed. You are under my command, and I shall act as if we were in the field. Obey my order, or, by Heaven, I'll kill you on the spot."

The man instantly submitted; and this decided the others, who were waiting the issue. Nor did they waver afterwards, though their sufferings increased every hour, and they lost their powers of endurance in proportion as they were most needed, men inured to hardship sinking under the cold and privation, and resigning themselves to death. The carpenter and first-mate became disabled, and a feeling of despair seized every breast, as days and nights succeeded each other and brought no prospect of relief. Starvation might be said to have begun, when a shout broke from the look-out on the cliff, and twenty voices echoed the cry—"A sail! a sail!"

CHAPTER 6

Before the Mast

It was three in the afternoon when the look-out descried the ship—a small schooner—just visible on the horizon; and already the sky lowered with a shade of night, which might prevent the beacon being seen. They felt all the misgivings of despairing men combating with hopes, and now doubted whether the signal would be understood, even if discerned. Who can imagine their feelings as they gazed on the distant sail, now thinking that she receded, now that she drew nearer, and straining their eyes for some token of recognition! The minutes seemed hours under this suspense. But soon they made out her hull and rig, and saw a streamer fly to her top. She was coming!

Such a cry rang out as she entered the bay and anchored, while her skipper waved his hat from the stern, and her crew gave a cheer, rushing aft to lower a boat. It came off with two men, but they were afraid to land as they saw the number of the castaways, who now all crowded to the water. Thus, they kept an oar's length, and seemed indisposed to take them off, when Lieutenant Douglas made a spring, and jumped into the boat, tumbling over them both. He then threw the painter to the others, who drew the boat ashore, and a load started for the schooner. The skipper admitted them onboard, though he hesitated about receiving so many, but finally yielded, as Douglas would not leave a man behind. He even sent for the mutineers, who had not seen the arrival, and took them off with the rest.

It appeared that the skipper had guessed the object of their beacon from being familiar with the coast, as he had visited it in his voyages to Great Jervis, where he traded for fish, and knew it to be uninhabited. To that settlement he was now bound, and he told them they must be content to remain there through the winter, as there would be no opportunity of leaving till the fishing-season expired. They had hoped that he might take them to Halifax, but were not in a position to make terms, and closed with his offer, all hurrying on board, and rejoicing together as the vessel bore them away.

They duly arrived at Great Jervis, and received the utmost kindness from the fishermen, who lived here amidst ice and snow, cut off from the world, and pursuing their calling amidst perpetual storms. There was some difficulty in providing them lodging, but the result verified the proverb that hinges the way on the will, and a roof was found for all. Lieutenant Douglas shared his cabin with Lieutenant Forbes, and they made room for the first mate and carpenter, whose crippled state excited their pity. Lieutenant Truscott and Ensign Bennett were carried some miles inland, in order to be placed under the care of a woman who was the physician of the settlement, and who ultimately restored them to health, either by her skill or nursing.

The party were almost naked on landing, having no clothes but those in which they escaped from the wreck, and which were in tatters from wear and exposure. But the settlement contained a store, where they found an assortment of slops, and Douglas rigged himself out as a sailor, donning the jacket and tarpaulin with as much pride as he had ever assumed his uniform. The place afforded scope for indulging his nautical tastes, and he spent the day in mingling with the fishermen, and sometimes sharing their pursuits. The long nights were heavy work, as they could obtain no books, and devise no amusements; but the convalescence of his guests improved his resources in this respect, as he could then practise navigation with the mate, and talk over mechanical problems with the carpenter.

But all grew weary of their detention at the settlement, and this put him on considering whether they might not try to reach Placentia, whence it would be easy to make their way to Quebec. He kept the project to himself for some time, fearing that it would be deemed chimerical, and thought it over and over again, as he paced to and fro on the cliff before his hut, looking down on the rocks and broken ice of Fortune Bay. The more he turned it in his mind, the more he felt disposed to put it in practice, and he determined to see what means existed for making the attempt.

The settlement maintained no communication with Canada, or any part of British America, but was visited in the spring by vessels from England, which came to exchange supplies for fish, and then sailed to different regions, chiefly the West Indies, Spain, Portugal, and the Mediterranean. They there bartered the fish for the productions of the soil, and carried these to England, where they found a ready market. The nearest point to America that he could hope to reach by such a channel was the West Indies, and he might be detained there an indefinite time, as no vessel would leave until the despatch of a convoy, and one so adventurous deemed it worth any risk to endeavour to make a direct passage.

He reminded his three messmates of these facts, and they talked them over together, when he broached his project of a dash, and they hailed it with rapture. He next enlisted a St. Lawrence pilot, brought off in a gale of wind the year before, and left at Fortune Bay, and he completed his number with a seaman from Newfoundland, who was anxious to leave the settlement, and whose knowledge of the coast would be of service.

It proved easier to obtain a crew than a vessel, but this was not beyond reach, and he met with a good fishing-boat, which the owner agreed to sell. The carpenter pronounced her adaptable, engaging to make her equal to the voyage, and Lieutenant Douglas became the purchaser; for he had no lack of means, as his bills on the authorities passed as money. They decided to rig the boat as a schooner, and set about her equipment, which furnished them with occupation during the short winter days, in that latitude so gloomy and depressing.

Its progress afforded Douglas the greatest pleasure, as he was fired by the prospect of carrying off his detachment in a vessel under his own command, and landing in triumph at St. John's. This banished from his mind all thought of the danger, and he longed for the moment when the weather would moderate, and permit oft their setting out. So early did he cherish his passion for distinction in the manner revealed in his maturer life, by seeking to excel in the performance of his duty rather than by bootless daring, though few found the same attraction in dangerous adventures.

The days that were not given to the schooner he spent in wandering round the coast or exploring the interior, sometimes in company with Lieutenant Forbes, but often alone; for his power of enduring cold and fatigue carried him where few could follow. And he felt that solitude heightened the sublimity of this wild outskirt of Nature, where rock upon rock started from the sea in fantastic shapes or prodigious boulders—*Pelion on Ossa*—and mountains rose to the clouds, or stood mantled in snow, frowning over precipices and chasms which gaped on valleys of granite, sending ravines into gloomy woods never pierced by the light of day. His mind had a poetic temper, though its habit was so practical, and such scenes left on it an impression that never faded.

The boat was completed for sea by April, but then came a succession of gales, which obliged them to defer setting out, and Douglas and Forbes spent the interval in a tour of the island. An incident happened in their absence that frustrated their whole plan. A storm drove into the harbour of St. Pierre a Newfoundland schooner, bound from Halifax to St. John's, and there the captain heard that a party of shipwrecked soldiers were detained at the fishing-station. He decided to go round to Fortune Bay and take them off, a lull in the weather permitting—for the shore was usually inaccessible at that season and even now was approached with danger.

His appearance brought out the whole population, who met him as he landed, and he made known his object, announcing that all must be on board within half an hour, as the sky and rising wind foretokened a tempest. This caused such excitement that no one thought but of himself, and some jumped into the boat at once, having nothing to carry away, and fearing to be left behind. It was not till the schooner was starting that the party missed Douglas and Forbes, and then they gathered round the captain, and entreated him to wait till a messenger could go to the hut and see if they had returned. With difficulty they brought him to consent, and the schooner hove to, while a boat pulled ashore, and one of the artillerymen started up the cliff, disappearing in an instant. But he returned alone; nothing could be heard of the two officers; and the schooner got under way.

This cruel necessity damped the joy of rescue; and eyes still watched the shore, as they moved through the water, unwilling to surrender the last hope. And now a gun flashed from the beach, as a signal that the absentees had appeared. They were seen to spring into a boat, which spread all sail, and came bounding through the waves, while the captain brought up and awaited her approach, cordially welcoming the two officers as they alighted on the deck.

The schooner hardly escaped from the shore before the gale broke; but the captain had no cause to regret his delay, since it secured him such a hand as Lieutenant Douglas. Nor had it involved much risk; for the weather improved towards morning, and then became fine, promising swift passage. But it did, not terminate without adventure; for they fell in with His Majesty's ship *Shark*, off Placentia, and were ordered to bring to and send a boat on board, as the crowd on deck excited suspicion. The yawl was hoisted up, and Lieutenant Douglas formed one of her crew, pulling the after-oar, the helm being taken by the captain.

The sea ran high, but they laid the boat alongside the frigate in dashing style, and the skipper ascended to the deck, while Douglas dropped astern to await his reappearance. He came within hail of the seamen in passing the main deck ports, and they called to him to leave a hand in the boat and jump up with the others to "have a jaw." He readily assented, and clambered in at a porthole, after securing the connivance of his companions by a wink, understood as implying that he was to appear as one of themselves. He met a kind welcome, and a shower of questions which naturally brought on the shipwreck, and those who have heard the story from his lips may imagine the fascination it exercised on the rough fellows gathered round.

The recital so absorbed eyes and ears that no one heeded a call from the captain's cabin for "Mr. Douglas," until the word passed to send aft the artillery officer who had come in the yawl, and Lieutenant Douglas now stepped out to obey, to the bewilderment of the circle, who fell back with exclamations of surprise, which merged in a general roar before he reached the cabin. He received a cordial greeting from Captain O'Brien, who commanded the frigate, and whom he found discussing a decanter of wine with his first lieutenant and the captain of the schooner.

The glass went round, and he heightened its enjoyment by explaining how he had come on board, and relating his adventure for'ard. This elicited a compliment to his appearance from Captain O'Brien, who said, "Your captain declares you are an excellent sailor, and you bear out his report." They spent a pleasant half-hour, and then bade each other goodbye, Lieutenant Douglas and the skipper returning in the yawl to the schooner, and the ships parting company.

The next day the schooner sighted St. John's, and stood into the harbour, where the crowded appearance of her deck attracted the notice of another man-of-war, which was lying at anchor, and she sent a boat to board her on her passage up. Thus, the captain found himself confronted by a lieutenant from His Majesty's ship *Pluto* before he scented the danger.

"Hilloa! what a number of hands you've got in this small vessel!" cried the lieutenant.

"Yes," was the reply.

"Where the —— did you find them?"

"I picked up the survivors of a shipwreck."

"Whew!" cried the lieutenant, in ecstasy; "What a glorious chance for us! We're short of hands, and can take them all. Just separate them from your crew; they couldn't have a better opening; for we're off to the West Indies tomorrow, and there'll be a swarm of prizes."

"But some of them are soldiers," interposed the skipper.

The lieutenant made a gesture intimating that such tales were not for his book. "Here's a sailor, at any rate," he said, slapping the shoulder of Lieutenant Douglas. "How long have you been at sea, my lad?"

"This is my first voyage on the ocean."

"Oh, bred in the coasting trade, eh?"

"Well, I know something of the coasting trade."

"I thought so. What craft?"

"The Berwick and Leith smacks."

"That will do—nothing better. Stand aside here!"

The young officer obeyed, with unmoved features, and was soon joined by others, who had been subjected to like inquiries. At length the lieutenant considered that he had made a good haul, and ordered the party to jump into the boat.

"I tell you there are soldiers in that lot," cried the skipper, thinking the joke had gone far enough; "and a soldier-officer, too."

"An officer!"

"Yes; that's him"—pointing to Lieutenant Douglas—"he's in the artillery."

The lieutenant laughed out, and referred the skipper to the marines, giving him to understand that he was a sailor, and knew a sailor, and that it would take a clever fellow to make him see an artillery officer in a lad rigged in sailor's slops, with figure to match. The skipper repeated his assertion, and he demanded to see the young man's commission, which obviously could not be produced, having gone to the bottom, and he now felt persuaded that the captain wished to cheat him out of his best man. He declared that he should carry off his party, and any claim to exemption must be made on the quarter-deck of the *Pluto*, where it could be fully investigated.

But he now met an unexpected check; for the skipper called his attention to the schooner's pendant, denoting that she sailed under a government charter, and this obliged him to sheer off disappointed, as he could not deny that it protected all on board.

His narrow escape from impressment did not deter Lieutenant Douglas from going ashore, and he and his friend Forbes landed together, after they had brushed their blue jackets and made a nautical toilet. Nor was this preparation without an object, as they had determined to pay their respects at Government House, and thither they repaired at once, and met the kindest reception from the governor, General Skinner.

They accepted an invitation to dinner, on the understanding that deficiencies should be excused, and made their appearance at the appointed hour in forecastle costume. The company included the captain of the *Pluto* and his smart lieutenant, who opened his eyes on seeing Douglas. But a knowing look set him at ease. The morning's adventure was not mentioned, and nothing interrupted the harmony of the evening. The *Pluto's* boat put the two artillerymen on board at a late hour, and the schooner sailed for Halifax at daybreak.

CHAPTER 7

Commanding a Cruiser

The commanding officer of the artillery at Quebec had been informed of the departure of the *Phillis* from Gravesend, and began to feel alarmed for her safety, as the time passed when she should have arrived. Hopes were entertained up to the close of the navigation, when her non-appearance was reported to Lord Dorchester, the Governor of Canada, and he requested the admiral commanding the squadron to ascertain if she had taken refuge in one of the seaports on the coast of Newfoundland, Cape Breton, or Nova Scotia; or whether there were any traces of her being wrecked on the Sable Bank. The search proved fruitless, and it was concluded that the *Phillis* had gone down at sea with all hands.

Such a disaster threw a gloom over the military community in British America, as many mourned the loss of comrades, not to mention nearer connexions; while their fate brought home to the mind the dangers of the passage, which each might himself be required to face at any moment. But soldiers forswear melancholy, and six months had almost effaced the impression, when a report spread of the arrival of a schooner with the survivors. This caused the greatest excitement, and the news was carried to His Royal Highness Prince Edward, who commanded the forces in Nova Scotia, and who instantly sent his *aide-de-camp* to bring up to his quarters any of the wrecked officers who might be in a state of health to attend.

Captain Wetherall returned with Douglas and Forbes, who were presented to His Royal Highness and received with the most gracious sympathy. The prince almost immediately inquired for Lieutenant Barnes, and learnt his fate with the deepest pain, knowing that he was an only son, and that the blow would be irreparable to his father, Colonel Barnes, to whom His Royal Highness was much attached.

He asked Lieutenant Douglas to relate the whole story of the ship-wreck, and listened with breathless interest, not concealing his emotion; and his kindness and sympathy made such an impression on the narrator, that he mentioned it to the author of this work sixty years after the occurrence.

His Royal Highness commanded both officers to dine with him in the evening, at the lodge, an honour they fully appreciated, but from which they seemed to be precluded by their limited wardrobe.

"Sir," said Lieutenant Douglas, after a moment's hesitation, "we have no clothes but what we stand in."

His Royal Highness could not repress a smile at the disclosure. "If all the tailors in Bond Street were here, I would receive you in no other dress," he said. "Come as you are."

Such a command was not to be disobeyed, and they only infringed it so far as to appear in clean check shirts, which they purchased for the occasion. His Royal Highness distinguished them by the kindest attention, though a large company was present, and requested Lieutenant Douglas to repeat his account of the shipwreck, after dinner, as he knew it would interest everybody. The prince sent his secretary on board the schooner next morning, to offer them and their companions surgical attendance, and whatever money, clothes, or other necessaries they might require; but they gratefully declined his bounty, having now drawn six months' pay, and being well-supplied.

The duty of recording these acts of the prince is most gratifying to the author of this work, who owes a personal debt to his memory, from the distinguished notice His Royal Highness took of his father, whom he selected from the whole army for the adjutancy of his own regiment, though the wear of hard service prevented his accepting the appointment.

Lieutenant Douglas and his companions left Halifax in a West India vessel carrying produce to Canada, and passed between Nova Scotia and the island of Cape Breton to the Gulf of St. Lawrence. Here they met a squall which sprung the fore-topmast, and compelled them to enter the bay to refit; affording the young officer an opportunity of visiting Douglas Town, erected to commemorate his father's relief of Quebec. The rescued party did not reach the capital till July. Here the name of Douglas was as familiar as at the town below, and would have insured the son of the great admiral a cordial reception at any time; but obtained him a heartier welcome now that he came as from the grave, seven months after his supposed loss. What gratified him most was the recognition of his meritorious conduct by his superiors—conveyed to him in the following letter from Lieut.-General Pattison, Commandant of the 4th Battalion of the Royal Artillery, and intended to acknowledge a narrative of the shipwreck he had addressed to Captain Frazer:—

To Lieutenant Douglas, 4th Battalion Royal Artillery.

(London), Hill-Street;

22nd April, 1796.

Dear Sir,

Your letter to Captain Frazer, reciting all the circumstances of your shipwreck, is a tale of such deep woe and distress as must necessarily make a forcible impression on the feelings of every-one who has read it. I am sure it had a full effect upon mine. It only remains for me to offer you my sincere congratulations on the providential escape which you and your surviving compan-ions most fortunately met with; and whilst I gratefully admire the ways of Providence in preserving your lives, I must at the same time pay *a just tribute to your cool, firm , and undaunted behav-iour* during the scenes of horror you underwent. *I am convinced that the prudent steps you took after getting on shore proved the happy means of your preservation.*

After the arrival of your letter I lost no time in laying it before the master-general, and, since that, I made the strongest appli-cation to the Board of Ordnance, requesting that they would be pleased to grant you and all the sufferers an indemnification for the losses sustained by that melancholy event, to which I yesterday received an answer, and which I transmit enclosed; although you will probably receive one directly from the board, requiring the affidavit therein specified. Unluckily I had not received this letter from the board when Lieutenant Kiggell called upon me yesterday, previous to his departure from Lon-don; but I hope this will reach him at Portsmouth before he sails; and that he may have the pleasure of giving it to you at Quebec.

I desire you will remember me with my good wishes to your young companions in the hour of distress, and accept the same yourself from, dear Sir,

Your very faithful humble servant,

James Pattison.

It will be seen that General Pattison ascribes the preservation of the survivors to the steps taken by Lieutenant Douglas, and the account of the occurrence must suggest the same conviction to every mind. At the age of nineteen he had shown an aptitude for grappling with difficulties, a degree of fortitude amidst privation and danger, and a power of influencing others, worthy of an experienced commander; and the manner in which his future life developed kindred qualities induces a regret that he had no opportunity of bringing them into play on the widest field.

The tribute paid to his conduct by General Pattison had an effect upon him similar to the recognition of his talents by Dr. Hutton in earlier years, encouraging his self-reliance without raising his self-esteem; and he used to say that the pleasure it afforded surpassed any he experienced from future appreciation. Nothing could show more the elevation of his character than this feeling, for he was to receive approval from the lips of kings; but he felt greater pride that the first trial had proved him worthy of his name, in a region connected with his father, and where it became him to, sustain his father's exploits.

The reputation he had acquired now obtained for him an employment of the very kind he could have wished. News reached Quebec that a French squadron was scouring the coast of Newfoundland, and had been seen bearing towards St. John's, sweeping before it the colonial traders and the vessels fishing on the great bank. Then came reports that it had not ventured to force the harbour of St. John's, but ran into the Bay of Bulls, where it destroyed the fishing stages, but made only a short stay, hurrying off to the northern entrance of the Gulf of St. Lawrence.

Here Admiral Richey hoisted the French flag on the island of St. Pierre, which had surrendered to a force from Halifax the year before, but had been left without a garrison, though a number of British fishermen had taken possession, and built a little town. This the French destroyed, as well as the fishing establishment and all the stages, leaving the island a desert. The squadron then divided, and a portion sailed for the coast of Labrador, to intercept the homeward-bound fleet from Quebec, while Admiral Richey remained near Cape Breton with four sail of the line and a frigate. The British naval force on the station consisted only of a 50-gun ship of an obsolete type, and four frigates, not one of which was in the St. Lawrence.

Hence the French admiral's vicinity excited great alarm at Quebec, and it became important to know what he was doing in the Gulf, particularly as the outward-bound fleet from England was due, and it appeared certain that it would be cut off. The situation of affairs determined the Canadian Government to send out a vessel for intelligence, and a schooner was equipped and got ready for the service, but so completely had the maritime class been absorbed by the war, that no competent person could be found to take her to sea.

In this emergency eyes began to be cast at a little sailing-boat which cruised about the bay in all weathers, but never more than when it blew fresh; and it transpired that she belonged to young Douglas, the hero of the shipwreck and the son of the admiral who relieved Quebec. A rumour spread that he had been in the navy, and this set the authorities to think that he was the very man they wanted and would make an excellent captain for their cruiser.

The subject came before the governor, General Prescott, and he sent the deputy adjutant-general to confer with Douglas, and ascertain his inclination, at the same time that he represented the importance of the service, and that it must be abandoned if not accomplished at once. It was too much to the taste of the young officer to be declined, but he set a modest appreciation on his own capacity, and only agreed to command the schooner if "no better man could be found." The governor declared that he wished for no better, and placed the vessel in his charge.

He might now feel rewarded for the self-denial he had practised in resigning the profession of his choice at the bidding of his guardians; for what more could he have achieved as a sailor than to be selected for such a post on the spot where he would most desire this recognition—in the basin of Quebec. Indeed, the navy would not have afforded such an opening at an age when he might still be a midshipman; and his success taught him that he could be in no better way to distinction if he made use of his opportunities.

The schooner was from 220 to 250 tons burthen, deep waisted in build, and reputed a swift sailer. Her armament consisted of eight 12-pounder carronades, and two long guns, in charge of artillerymen, and she carried a good crew with a first and second mate, and a pilot for the passage down the river. She set sail about the middle of September, proceeding to the island of Bic, where her commander took measures to prevent pilots boarding strange vessels, and arranged for the transmission of intelligence to the seat of government. He vividly remembered the incidents of the expedition to his latest years, taking pride in relating them to the few whom he entertained with his adventures, and no one who had been much at sea could resist the animation with which he described his mode of handling the schooner.

It was necessary that he should make himself acquainted with her best points, in order that he might bring them out in the event of being chased by the French fleet, and he tried her on every tack, whence he found that she carried a tight weather helm, coming to the wind readily, and making a long short directly to windward, with the helm amidships, when not impeded by her square topsails. Then she easily paid off with the fore-staysail sheet close hauled to windward, and helped a little with the jib, and never fell off after tacking. He avoided using the topsails when close hauled on turning to windward, except in very light winds, always working the vessel under her fore and aft sails.

The experience he acquired of her weatherly qualities determined him to approach the French fleet from the windward, should it fall in his way, for he was satisfied that no square-rigged ship could give him chase on that course, whatever the direction of the wind, and he cared little about receiving a shot or two if he could get sufficiently near to ascertain whether the ships carried troops. Hence, he denied himself the gratification of hoisting a pendant, as this might put them on the alert, and the schooner sailed under the usual merchant ensign displayed at the main peak.

They passed the first night of her voyage above Crane Island, where they came to anchor, and Lieutenant Douglas turned in, after giving orders that he should be called at high water. This brought him on deck before daylight, and he immediately loosed sail, and set to heaving up anchor. But here he met a difficulty of an unexpected kind, as if to put him on trial, for the ordinary purchase had no effect in moving the anchor. The handspikes were double manned with the same result, and the mate recommended cutting it adrift.

But he could not be reconciled to this sacrifice, the vessel having no spare bower-anchor, and he had been in danger enough to learn the value of such a provision; so he determined to persevere, and ordered a tackle to be fixed round the cable, and taken to the windlass, on which the men again heaved up, and the anchor came away. But there was still a strain, and the cause plainly appeared on catting, as the fluke was found to have hooked in the ring of another and larger anchor, which it brought up from the bottom, in a condition that showed it had been lying there many years. The incident exhibited the character of Douglas in one of its strong points, his tenacity of purpose, and had an inspiring effect on the crew, who were now ready to follow him wherever he led.

A light wind accompanied the schooner for a time, but left her off Gruse Island, where it fell calm, and Douglas perceived a change in the colour of the water, as if it had shallowed. The pilot declared it was of great depth, but he retained his opinion, and ordered soundings, which reported only twenty-six fathoms. The chart was now produced, and corroborated the pilot, showing no bank, so he laid one down on the spot, marking it by the bearings of two headlands which stood pretty distant, and it proved a valuable discovery. He tested its worth himself, for he instantly threw out a span of hooks baited with pork, and hauled up two splendid cod. The line was sent down again and again, and upwards of a hundred fish were caught while they drifted over. A number were split and salted, and afterwards distributed by Lieutenant Douglas among the merchants and fishmongers of Quebec, who established a fishery near the bank in the following year, and it may be in operation to the present time.

Off Ante Costi Island the schooner sighted a large square-rigged vessel, coming up under a press of sail, and the pilot declared her to be the *Caroline*, a well-known craft in the Quebec trade. This emboldened Lieutenant Douglas to carry on after the usual signals, and he then hoisted his pendant and fired a gun. The stranger shortened sail, but apparently with some confusion, and eyes in the schooner began to peer at her more narrowly. But the pilot insisted that she was the *Caroline*, and spoke so positively that Douglas launched the jolly-boat, determined to go on board, and see if he could obtain intelligence of the fleet.

Strange appearances came out as the boat advanced, and he ordered the men to lay on their oars till he took a better look. All the officers of the ship, were standing abaft, the deck was crowded for'ard, and some heads in the waist showed the red cap of the French Revolutionists. But any misgivings these excited were dispelled by the captain, who presented himself at the side of the ship, and requested Douglas to come alongside, declaring that all was right, that the vessel was the *Caroline*, and that he was the bearer of important intelligence. The rowers gave way, a rope was thrown, and Douglas jumped on board.

He almost started back as he looked round and saw a strong barricade of timber across the deck, and a carronade pointed for'ard through a porthole in each waist. But these mysterious appearances were now explained, and he learned that the *Caroline* had been chartered to bring out three hundred French prisoners, who volunteered for the second battalion of the 60th, in garrison at Quebec; and the party had conspired to rise on the crew during the voyage, and carry her into a French port. The scheme was discovered, and the captain took precautions against surprise by erecting the barricade, which gave him the control of the Frenchmen, whom he compelled to work the sails for'ard on pain of being shot down, while they were only permitted to appear on deck in certain numbers.

Thus the ship crossed the Atlantic; and her preservation seemed the more wonderful as she had fallen in with the homeward-bound Quebec fleet on the coast of Labrador, and they had been attacked by the French squadron, when she alone escaped. The captain heard from fishermen that he would meet another French squadron in the Gulf of St. Lawrence, but afterwards discovered that it had gone north and joined the sister force off the Banks of Newfoundland, where they had been seen bearing away together; and this was the intelligence he wished to forward to Quebec.

Douglas lost no time in carrying it on, and it spread through the city, dispelling the apprehension of an attack on Canada, as it established the fact that a fleet of seven sail of the line and three frigates had been sent out for no other object than a raid. He received the thanks of the Canadian Government for having undertaken so difficult a service, and performed it so successfully, while his praises were repeated on every side, and he found himself a popular hero before he was twenty.

The winter of 1796 passed very gaily, and every house was open to the young officer who had so well sustained his father's fame. In the spring he was invited to a public banquet given by the Volunteers who had taken up arms for the defence of the city in the campaign of 1776, and intended to celebrate the anniversary of its relief by Sir Charles. He met an enthusiastic reception, and his name was coupled with the toast of the day, eliciting his first speech. No fragment of this oration has survived; but he used to recite a *stanza* of a poem composed for the occasion by a Presbyterian minister who had been chaplain to the Scottish corps during the siege, and which acclaimed the exploit of his father. The lines will not be out of place here:—

With freedom, peace, and plenty blest,
Protected by Britannia's sway,
Secure we sing of dangers past,
And hail the sixth of May,
The glorious sixth of May:
Brave Douglas, wafted on the gale,
Did anchor in the bay.

CHAPTER 8

Among the Indians

In May, 1797, Lieutenant Douglas was ordered to Upper Canada, in command of a detachment of artillery consisting of two officers and a considerable number of men, who were to relieve a like force at Kingston. The movements of the troops were then all effected by water; but there was no chain of canals, as at present, the only one in existence being higher up, at the Falls; and the boats had to be rowed up the river from Quebec, a service for which the troops were regularly trained, and at which they were very expert.

The detachment embarked in Canadian *bâteaux*, each provided with two voyageurs, a headsman and sternman; for the steering was conducted at both ends, being carried on with paddles in deep water, and long poles in shallow, or by dragging the boat by tow-lines where there was a path. The party landed at night and bivouacked on the banks—a mode of travelling very agreeable to its commander, as it afforded him leisure to contemplate the scenery. This was of a character to strike an imagination so attracted by adventure, for the mighty stream bore him through forest and prairie, morasses and savannas, such as he had never conceived; while behind rose towering heights, sometimes backing a settler's clearing, but oftener the *wigwams* of Indians, almost the only tenants of these solitudes. The voyage occupied a month, but he never found it irksome, and felt no elation at the sight of Kingston, where they arrived towards the end of June.

He had reason to be satisfied with the situation of the town, breasting Lake Ontario, which gave a scope to his nautical habits; and the facilities it afforded were not neglected. During the summer he was constantly afloat, crossing the lakes in sailing vessels, or coasting along in boats, often going a distance in his Indian canoe spearing salmon by torchlight, or led by his adventurous spirit into the woods. Here he roamed about with Indians, living in their *wigwams*, and joining them in deer-stalking, shooting, fishing, and other pursuits. His adventures carried him where few white men had penetrated, and were sometimes attended with danger.

On one occasion he was fishing in a stream, when he felt something cold strike his leg, and found his foot on the neck of a rattlesnake, which had coiled itself above his ankle. It might be imagined that his first idea would be how to effect his escape; but how to prevent the escape of the rattlesnake was all his care. Izaak Walton never played more dexterously with a trout than he set to work on this object. He wished to "catch him alive;" and this required instant action as well as adroitness, while he seemed without any means of proceeding. But he had learnt the arts of the Indians, and now put them in practice, applying them with the same facility. Keeping his foot still, he broke a branch from a tree within reach, tore down the bark, and made it into a string, one end of which was left fast to the branch, while the other formed a noose, which he slipped round the rattlesnake as he sprang aside, and caught it up dangling from the stick, carrying it home uninjured.

The bite of the rattlesnake is usually considered fatal; but he heard from the Indians that the plantain-leaf is an antidote, and once saw its efficacy proved. He was out hunting rattlesnakes with an Indian, when his companion was bitten, and looked very disturbed for a moment, but then caught sight of a plantain, and this set him at rest. To apply the remedy was the work of an instant. He drew out his knife, scarified the bite, and then covered it with plantain-leaves, which he had first chewed into a pulp, swallowing the juice. A few days healed the wound, and it gave no further trouble. Douglas remarked that the plantain grew profusely where rattlesnakes were most common.

It seems a contradiction that one so addicted to the wildest adventures should find attraction in the gentle art of angling. Yet Walton himself was not a more ardent fisherman; and he was ready to start with his rod at any hour whether of the day or night. Nor does his passion for the quiet sport appear incongruous if we remember that it exacts alertness; for this ministered to his activity, though not employing it, while it left him free to meditate. Thus, it remained his diversion in later years; and some of the old chiefs of our army recall their instructor by the side of the little stream at Sandhurst more familiarly than in any other situation.

His roving habits could not escape notice in so small a community, and now brought him again before the Canadian authorities, who were looking for a person to head a mission to the Cherokees, a tribe of Indians expelled from the United States for its British sympathies, and which they had located on Lake Erie. They learnt that Lieutenant Douglas possessed just the experience needed, and hastened to place the mission under his charge, remembering his good service in their cruiser. The party consisted of two or three other officers, an interpreter, and a few Canadian woodsmen; and the object in view was to induce the Cherokees to forego some obnoxious customs which gave occasion for scandal.

The matter required to be handled with delicacy, and the way was to be smoothed by presents, as the chief of the Cherokees stood upon his dignity, and guarded it with a tomahawk reputed to take off scalps with artistic precision. But he received the mission with great courtesy, and pledged himself to every demand as soon as he understood that they brought him a supply of rum. This was one of the presents that Lieutenant Douglas intended to hold back till his departure; but the Indians baffled his vigilance, and seized it by stealth, carrying it off to the chief's *wigwam*, where they immediately began a carouse. Later in the day they paid a visit of ceremony to the mission in a very unceremonious way, and a state unsuited both to ceremony and business. Hence, they were not invited to partake of refreshment, which they considered an insult, and seemed disposed to resent, going away very sulky.

Their manner caused the white men an uneasy feeling; but it gradually wore off, and they sat down to dinner after a scout had gone down the village, and brought back a report that it appeared quiet. But his intelligence proved delusive; for they had hardly begun their meal when the blanket in the doorway was dragged aside, and the Indians reappeared, now all armed, and looking ferocious, but stalking in without speaking in their usual, single file.

The chief displayed his famous tomahawk; but how it took off scalps with such nicety seemed to puzzle some of the Canadians, for they eyed it dubiously, as if they would prefer their scalps left on till he produced a more efficient instrument. He was not in a mood to respect such scruples, but drew his men round the table in a threatening manner, and as steady a line as their topweight of rum would permit—all being done so quickly that no opposition could be organised, and everyone kept his seat, feeling that a movement might provoke attack.

The silence was broken by the chief, who harangued his men; and Douglas noticed that the Canadian interpreter looked graver as he proceeded, which led him to inquire the cause, and he learnt that the chief was dwelling on the affront of the morning, and claiming vengeance. The Indians needed little incitement; for they now broke into a low chant, and moved slowly round the table, waving their tomahawks above their heads, and leaving no doubt of their intentions. Douglas gave a hint to his companions, and they all snatched their knives from the table, and sprang into the clear side of the hut, where they planted their backs to the wall and awaited attack. But their manoeuvre disconcerted the Indians, who also came to a stand, and looked over at the white men with an air of bewilderment. Then the chief demanded the meaning of this display—protested that he meant nothing uncivil himself—and led his warriors out of the hut, leaving the Canadians with their scalps untouched, but not much disposed to finish their dinner.

They deemed it prudent to keep quiet for the rest of the day, and no one ventured forth; but Douglas felt reassured as the day closed and they saw nothing of the Indians. It is difficult to remain indoors in America in the early nights of Fall, when the fresh air comes sweeping through the forest or over the mountain-side, and the sky is radiant with stars. The young officer slipped out, and turned up a path towards the wood, looking now at the spangled heavens, now at the darkened landscape, only visible in its outlines. He was so free from fear that he had come out unarmed, and wandered carelessly on, thinking of anything but danger. But his ear had become so quickened by training that it caught the slightest sound, and now attracted him to a tree close by, where he saw a dark object, which be made out to be an Indian.

The man started out and stood right in his path, laying his hand on his shoulder as he came up, and uttering a cry like a horse's neigh, but more shrill and piercing. This is the Indian mode of giving a challenge, and Douglas responded with a blow, which caught the savage between the eyes, and rolled him in the dust, where he sprawled a moment and then crawled off in a manner that the victor used to describe as "going away like a snake." He saw him no more, and returned to the hut without further adventure.

A few days of his management brought the Indians to a better disposition, and the chief of the mission and the chief of the Cherokees became such fast friends that they afterwards travelled together into the backwoods, and visited some of the distant tribes. Douglas represented to the Canadian Government that his friend should be rewarded for the services he had rendered to England, and this obtained for him a pension, (this anecdote was related to the author by General Sir Hew Ross, G.C.B.), which had such an effect on his habits that the famous tomahawk went out of practice, and the settlers had no better neighbour than Joseph Brandt, the chief of the Cherokees.

One of the distant tribes introduced Douglas to a young white girl, who had been living amongst Indians from her infancy, when a party of warriors ravaged a settlement and carried her off. He describes her as being "beautiful as possible," and a great favourite with the Indians, all the tribe paying her deference. But the example she offers of the influence of beauty over savages is not surprising, and we may wonder more at what he records of the influence of savage life on herself; for a strange chance discovered her to her brother, and he entreated her to return home, but she refused, declaring that she was perfectly happy, and could not support a different existence. Lieutenant Douglas remarks, in the old note-book which preserves this anecdote:

> Feelings and happiness being unknown, a kind of contented apathy succeeds.

These adventures might seem unproductive for future use. But such an impression would be erroneous, for they formed an admirable training for a soldier—inuring him to privation and fatigue, exercising his self-reliance, and quickening and developing his invention by the constant demand for stratagem and contrivance. These were qualities in which he came to excel, and his wanderings taught him other lessons of value in his profession. He surveyed the country with a military eye, learnt how its features were used in desultory warfare, and thus convinced himself that undisciplined men might carry on a struggle against regular troops if they were properly handled. We shall see that this knowledge proved serviceable at a later period of his life.

His activity knew no limit, and he practised athletic feats on the ice when winter shut him out from the water. His power of enduring fatigue was marvellous. On one occasion he wished to be present at a ball at Quebec, and skated the whole way from Montreal, in company with a brother officer. The achievement cost his companion his life, but it made no impression on himself, and he attended the ball, and returned to Montreal as hale as he set out. (For this anecdote the author is indebted to Colonel Basil Jackson.)

CHAPTER 9

Roughing it Home

The death of his half-brother Charles called Lieutenant Douglas to England in the autumn of 1798, and he obtained leave of absence, hoping to reach Quebec for a passage by the Fall fleet. But he arrived too late, and had determined to make his way home by Boston or New York, when he heard of an opportunity of proceeding by a little brig which had failed to complete her crew and cargo in time to accompany the fleet, and was now on the point of sailing. He hurried on board, and found a rough north-country skipper, who agreed to give him a berth if he would put up with the accommodation; and the beginning of November saw him running down the St. Lawrence on his way home.

The brig was laden with timber, and mustered a running crew—so called from a practice during the war of engaging hands to carry a vessel to port—and the young officer might think that a winter-passage did not promise well under such auspices, particularly after his adventures in the voyage out. But he enjoyed a little roughing, took things in a cheerful way, and made himself as useful as agreeable, so that the captain discovered he was both a valuable help and a pleasant companion. He felt all the animation of high spirits in the flush of youth, and could spin a yarn of a quality to make the forecastle stare, while he sang all Dibdin's songs, and danced a hornpipe.

His qualifications in sailorcraft would have rated him A.B. in any ship afloat; for he could haul, reef, and steer, heave the log and cast the lead, make points and gaskets, form grummets, splice the main brace, mend ropes of the running rigging with the long splice, and the standing rigging with the short; make all kinds of knots, whether reef or single and double bend, close hitch, or bowling knots; and point ropes with unequalled neatness. His friends well remember how he gloried in these accomplishments when his literary and scientific attainments received no allusion, and he said nothing of the productions which had been translated into every language of Europe. His nautical knowledge was all needed for the voyage now in progress, and proved of the greatest service.

The third morning out brought an increase of wind, but no appearance of bad weather, and the captain and his passenger went to their berths at night, leaving the brig in charge of the mate. Lieutenant Douglas soon fell asleep, but was awoke by a violent lurch, and found the vessel pitching about in a way that he could not account for, though allowing for a gale of wind which could be heard roaring above. He felt so uneasy that he threw on his clothes and rushed to the deck, where his first glance made him call out for the mate, and the helmsman answered that he had gone below.

The brig was in a trough of the sea, staggering under single-reefed topsails, with the maintop-gallant sail set, and the jib and fore and aft mainsail, while the wind blew nearly abeam; Douglas saw that they could only be saved from foundering by instant action, and he snatched a marline-spike from the windlass, ran to the fore-batch, and gave the well-known taps which call up all hands.

He then shouted to the watch to stand by the top-gallant braces and haulyards, and ease off the weather-haul upon the lee-brace. The company now came tumbling up, and he ordered them to let go the haulyards and sheets as the sail shook and clew up the top-gallant sail. Two boys started aloft, and the sailors instinctively obeyed his orders, without considering how he came to be in command.

As swiftly as he spoke, the top-gallant sail was handed, the jib hauled down, the tacks of the mainsail hauled up, the topsail braces manned, the weather fore-topsail brace rounded to, and the lee eased off, and the weather main topsail brace eased off, and the lee rounded to. The uproar roused the captain, and he came on deck in time to hear the final order—"Lower away the topsail; haul up the reef-tackle; watch, away up; reef the main topsail!" The brig was safe!

The captain had stood speechless in this crisis, but now seized his passenger's arm, and asked for the mate. Douglas replied by describing how he had come on deck, and the position in which he had discovered the ship, but the mate he knew nothing about. His name was called in vain, and Douglas thought that one of the heavy lurches of the ship might have pitched him overboard; but the captain had other misgivings, and ordered a search. It turned out as he suspected, and the mate was found stretched between his chest and the bilge of the ship's side, helplessly drunk. The captain paced the deck for a moment after this discovery, and then suddenly brought the ship to the wind on the other tack.

"I am sorry for your disappointment," he said to Douglas, "but I must return to Quebec, and lay the brig up for the winter,"

"On what account?" asked the young officer with surprise.

"You see I can't trust the mate; and how can I undertake a winter's voyage across the Atlantic without one?"

"Well, you have complimented me on my activity and seamanship. Stand on your voyage, and I'll take charge of the mate's watch, if you'll accept of my services, I assure you, you may trust me far beyond what you have seen. At least I shall never get drunk; nor will I ever leave the deck while you are below; and I promise to do nothing important during my watch without consulting you, until you have more experience of my abilities."

No proof of his efficiency could be needed after such a trial, and the skipper closed with the offer on the spot without disguising his satisfaction. The brig was put on her old course, and the new mate took up his duties by remaining on deck till the next watch.

The situation met both his tastes and wants; It enabled him to indulge his love of sailoring and gather fresh experience, while it opened to him a field for exertion which he had begun to miss. He now found an object for the energy he had expended on boatings and skatings, in wanderings in the backwoods and adventures with the Indians, and derived more pleasure from its exercise.

Nor was it immaterial that he came into closer relations with men of humble stamp, for this taught him to appreciate merit in whatever rank it might appear. Indeed, all the early part of his life tended to expand his perceptions in this respect, and raised him above any prejudice of caste, so that no one could be less influenced by pride of birth or station. Indeed, his pride was to feel that he had made his own position, and it was his ambition to be valued for himself, not to shine by his lineage or title, nor by the honours on his breast. He once said to his biographer:

I don't belong to the aristocracy, and am satisfied to be one of the people.

Nor did the author suspect his descent from the great Douglas, till he came to write his biography.

Daylight brought an improvement in the weather, and a severe cold knocked up the captain, keeping him below, and increasing the responsibilities of his deputy. These were the more onerous, as he had to navigate the ship by dead reckoning, the gloom rendering it impossible to take an observation. Thus, he pursued a course for three days in anxiety and doubt, hardly venturing to leave the deck. At last the sun gave a promise of peering out. He ran down for the captain's sextant, caught a momentary gleam, and ascertained the position of the ship. Soon afterwards the weather cleared up; the captain became convalescent, and his troubles ceased, leaving him at ease for the rest of the voyage.

A fair wind carried the brig to Greenock, and they reached the anchorage in the twilight of a winter's morning, which threw a dimness over the shore, as its outlines rose to view. They had now to shorten sail, and Douglas called out the order, when he missed five of the best hands, rendering it difficult to work the ship. He complained to the captain, who was standing by, but received a signal to be silent, and presently heard a boat grate alongside; a boathook grappled the gangway, and a pressgang scrambled on deck.

"Hilloa! you're short-handed here," said their chief.

"It seems we are," answered the captain, looking round.

"Oh! you don't know? Well, let's see the payroll of your crew."

The book was produced, and overhauled.

"One—two—four; you're five short! Below, eh?"

"I wish you may find 'em," replied the captain. "The rascals have left us to do the work; and I doubt have got off in some of the shore boats, for we've had several board us, as we came up."

The pressgang replied to this speech in strong language, intimating a low opinion of the captain's veracity, and spread over the brig, searching hole and corner. But no skulkers turned up, and they were obliged to go off balked. Douglas rubbed his eyes as they vanished in the distance, for the five missing men had reappeared on deck, and were composedly chewing their quids. His bewilderment amused the captain, who took him below and disclosed a recess between the after-cabin and his own berth, formed by a bulkhead, and so contrived that the door of the berth could not be opened without covering the entrance. It just afforded room for half-a-dozen men to stand shoulder to shoulder, and here the absentees had taken refuge.

The time was now come for parting. Lieutenant Douglas had more than satisfied the captain, and brought the rough sailor to appreciate his character as well as his seamanship. They bade each other an affectionate farewell, and the young officer hastened to join his family. But the separation pressed heavily on the sailor, and he thought that one with such a leaning to the sea might be tempted to give up the military profession and return to the cabin; so he wrote to him in this strain, making him a most liberal offer, little short of putting him in his own place. At the same time, he dwelt on the dangers they had met together, and the pleasant hours they had passed, while he pointed out that the sea was the natural field for the son of a great admiral, and his own favourite element.

Such a proposal might have seemed ridiculous to a young man of family, in the situation of Lieutenant Douglas, already a noted officer and likely to win high rank. But the heart it addressed never denied a response to good feeling, however displayed, and he saw only the pathos of the captain's offer, not its absurdity. He studied how to decline it in a way that would give no wound; and this led him to reply in a poetic epistle, which paid a tribute to the sailor's calling, declaring that it would have been his choice if duty had not made him a soldier—that he must now return to his profession, but should never forget either the dangers they had shared, or their convivial hours—and that he wished nothing but prosperous gales to the *Favourite!* There is no copy of the effusion amongst his papers; but he once recited it to his biographer, and it struck him as breathing the very spirit of Dibdin.

CHAPTER 10

Training Generals

Lieutenant Douglas had not been long in England before he fell under the yoke of matrimony, and became the husband of Miss Anne Dundas, daughter of James Dundas, Esq., of Edinburgh, a lady in her nineteenth year, and who was to prove that beauty is not always ephemeral, for in her it seemed unfading. But the personal attractions of Mrs. Douglas were her least merit; it was in her amiable qualities that she excelled; and these made her loved in the social circle, while she was venerated in that of her family. It may certainly be affirmed that no one ever fulfilled more tenderly the duties of wife and mother.

The young officer obtained his company in October, 1799, and was transferred to the 5th battalion, in which he became adjutant. Hence, he passed to the horse artillery, and was placed in command of the Mortar Brigade. Both positions afforded him opportunities of extending his professional experience: the one by accustoming him to manoeuvre a larger body of artillery than is often brought into action; the other by opening up a different range of evolutions and practice, consequent on the force being mounted. Meanwhile he strengthened his practical knowledge by study, and spent some years in thus perfecting himself in his profession, till he obtained the reputation of being one of the most scientific officers in the army.

The British service did not stand high for science at this time. A great minister had said that an English general meant an old woman in a red riband; while a story was current of an English soldier who told his French captors they had nearly made a prisoner of his commander, and elicited the reply—"Ah! we know better than that: he does us more good at the head of your army." Such jibes effected what could not be accomplished by disasters, and the discovery was made that an officer would be all the more efficient for a professional education. Hence arose the Royal Military College, established at High Wycombe, and placed under the supervision of General Jamy, who had been *aide-de-camp* to Frederic the Great. The post of superintendent of the Senior Department was offered to Captain Douglas.

The field presented to his talents in the artillery opened to him such prospects that he did not respond to the overture, however he might be gratified by the selection. But the mischief caused by ignorant staff officers had been so apparent in Holland that the Duke of York determined to secure his co-operation in the movement, as the best instructor the army could supply, and he tempted him with contingent advantages.

He first proposed to give him a brevet majority in the artillery, but this was thought likely to create "uneasiness," and met an opponent in the master-general, Lord Chatham, though he declared himself willing to recommend "His Majesty to prevail on Captain Douglas to retire from the artillery," with the rank of major in the line. (Letter from the Earl of Chatham to the Duke of York, in the *Douglas Papers*.) His Majesty intimated his wishes accordingly; and Captain Douglas received notice of his appointment from General Harcourt, the governor, on the 4th January, 1804. (Letter from General Harcourt, in the *Douglas Papers*.)

Major Douglas did not leave Woolwich without an adventure, which displayed his ingenuity and adroitness, no less than his courage. The severe weather had frozen over Bowater's Pond, on Woolwich Common, and a party of officers were skating and sliding round the sides, when Lieutenant W. M. Smith ventured over the bound, and the ice gave way, precipitating him into the water. He came to the surface two or three times, and caught at the ice round the hole, but it broke in his clutch, and its thinness prevented any one going to his assistance. Major Douglas heard an outcry, and hastened to the spot.

Instantly he ordered the soldiers standing round to pick up some wattles that were lying on the banks, and push them over towards the hole, thus forming a sort of gangway; and on this he extended himself, caught Lieutenant Smith as he was sinking, and dragged him out of the water. The wattle bore their weight, and he succeeded in drawing him to the bank, amidst the congratulations of the spectators. (This anecdote has reached the author from Lieut.-General Sir Frederic Smith, M.P., the nephew of the rescued officer, who was present.)

Another day he was attracted by a crowd in the street, and found a drunken man lying on the ground, crying out, and moving his arms and legs as if swimming. He saw that he was one of the party who had been with him in the shipwreck, and touched his arm, when the man looked up, giving him a vacant stare.

"Where were you on that night?" asked Major Douglas.

The man sobered in a moment "I was by your side, sir, hanging on by the shrouds," he answered.

"Well, it's all over," returned Major Douglas; "you must be quiet now."

He sent him to a lodging, and tried to place him in comfort, paying for his maintenance, but nothing could keep the poor fellow from drink, and it drove him mad. He lingered in this state for a time, and then died.

The army dates an era from Major Douglas's appointment to the Military College; for he supplied it with a new class of officers, who made it able to "go anywhere and do anything." The training hand was unseen, but its work was apparent everywhere, and nowhere more than in the staff of Wellington. Our commanders have borne the same impress down to our own time, and it has been signalised by Hardinge, Gomm, Simpson, and Brown in our latest struggles on the fields of India and the Crimea.

Rugby has canonised Dr. Arnold, who cast the slough from the teacher's office, and raised it to a ministry. Major Douglas achieved the same result on a rougher field, cultivating the minds of grown men who were versed in the uses of the world and the camp. He brought knowledge down to the humblest ability, and advanced it to a point that satisfied the highest, at the same time raising the moral tone of the students by keeping before them the example of his own conduct. No part of the task of preparing this volume has been so interesting to its author as the perusal of the letters addressed to him by the officers thus moulded, writing from every clime, and often from the very scene of battle, and whose names are among the proudest in our military annals.

Fond glances are here thrown back at the circle at Wycombe from the midst of the big wars, the pleasant hours spent there are remembered on the bed of suffering, and the presence of the teacher is felt a thousand miles away; for more than one of the writers obtains the approval of his superiors through carrying out his suggestions; others write to remind him that they owe their position to his good offices; and others accidentally discover that he was their friend, when they have long held their appointments. One incident of this kind is touchingly brought out. A Mr. Deane writes to inform him of the death of his son, who had passed through the college and then obtained an appointment under the Duke of Gloucester, and he relates that the duke had surprised him with the information that the post had been given to his son on the recommendation of Major Douglas.

He pathetically adds:

> You will easily imagine the feelings which agitated the mind of an afflicted father.

Then he begs him to accept some of his son's books, "in remembrance of one who cherished the greatest respect and esteem for you." Another letter is from a Lieutenant Thorne, who asks him for a certificate of his conduct while at the college, and what he thinks of the possibility of his obtaining a company without purchase. The reply of Major Douglas enclosed a letter from Colonel Gordon, acknowledging the receipt of his "particular recommendation of Lieutenant Thorne of the Buffs," and stating that it had been laid before the commandeer-in-chief, who had ordered Lieutenant Thorne to be noted for promotion.

Captain, (afterwards General), Sir Philip Bainbrigge, writes to inform him of his being placed on the quartermaster-general's staff, which he learns at the Horse Guards is "in consequence of the favourable report you were kind enough to make of me." Another of the officers who thus thanks him for his first employment on the staff is Captain, (afterwards Lord) Hardinge.

He was as alert to check vice as to promote merit, and gave a reality to the phrase of "officer and gentleman," which became characteristic with all under his command. His consistency on this point is instanced in a draft of a letter to an officer at the college, amongst his papers, and it would be hard to adduce a case in which authority tempered firmness with more kindness and delicacy. The letter disclaims any right to interfere in the defaulter's private affairs, but warns him that he cannot be allowed to bring discredit on the college, and insists on his paying the debts he had incurred while there, and conforming to all the rules. He upheld the same standard on every occasion. An officer under his command might be sure of never being watched, but he was called up at once if he obtruded irregularities, and learnt that military liberty did not extend to licence, and never forgot honour.

Such was Howard Douglas, in the flower of his life—the guardian of virtue, the kind fosterer of merit, and above anything mean or little.

Few can rejoice at the promotion of others, when kept in fee background themselves, or even when themselves advancing; but here was one who took a pleasure in helping others forward, and often did it by stealth, while he seemed destined to toil unknown, charged with the part of effecting a great work, which would never reveal the workman. But this engaged all his energies, though it did not satisfy his ambition. He panted for action, but his withers were unwrung. To repeat the words of the chaplain-general, "his mind was too full of higher things to have space for envy or bitterness."

He was content to drudge on, not living only for himself, but for his country and age, though conscious of his own military genius, requiring but an opening to win distinction. His feelings are apparent in the interest he evinces in his pupils after they have left his charge; and they write to him in a strain that recognises the tie, and seeks its continuance. Nothing could mark the impression he made upon them more, except the pride they show in each other, for these men of war seem imbued with his spirit, when we see them glorying in every success of a "Wycombite," and preserving the friendships they formed under his eyes through a hundred battles.

It must not be supposed that he found his work at the college all smooth, or pursued it without opposition. New ideas are distrusted by military authorities, and the notion in favour at the moment was to fight by manoeuvres, in imitation of Frederic of Prussia, the idol of his old *aide-de-camp*, Jamy. But Major Douglas looked for instruction to passing operations, and from these learnt a different lesson. He had seen the Duke of York and the Austrian commanders carry on war by rule, and always unsuccessful, while the French generals had won victories against rule, and brought the finest manoeuvres to grief. This led him to perceive that the art of war rested on the simplest principles, and that success resulted from their application. His theory was what Napoleon afterwards bruited, when declaring that victory remained with the strongest battalions; and he taught that strategy consisted in massing the greatest force at the vital point, and striking before it could be succoured. We shall see him venturing to give this counsel to the Great Captain, and hear Wellington exclaim "Douglas was right," when a different course forced him to retreat.

The mode he adopted of teaching military sketching, reconnoitring, and surveying, was an improvement so obvious that it could not be resisted; but he only succeeded in introducing other changes after long delays. The following extract from a letter which he received in

1806 from General Harcourt, shows what obstacles he had to surmount, and how they cramped his usefulness:—

> I shall be very anxious to know whether you have made a convert of General Jamy to your ideas for the improvement of your model, though, however desirable it may be to have the approbation of so scientific a person, I confess I am so strongly impressed with the utility of the plan proposed, that, if necessary, it shall have my full support towards carrying it into execution. Your proposal for instructing the students in the principle and construction of military bridges, and the general uses of artillery, deserves every encouragement; and although you may occasionally suffer mortification from the illiberality of one individual and the prejudices of another, I am persuaded your zeal will not be diminished in a matter where the improvement of the establishment is so much concerned.

No doubt it was cheering to possess the confidence of the governor, and encouraging to have his support, but he detested contention, and must have been under constant harass. His temper could bear the strain, but a check in the performance of his duty was felt; for he had no interest in view but the public service, and liked this to be acknowledged. His open nature let his feelings be seen, and General Harcourt knew the chord to touch in order to sustain him in his efforts:

> I am persuaded your zeal will not be diminished in a matter where the improvement of the establishment is so much concerned.

Such an assurance gave the support he most coveted, for it recognised his disinterestedness as well as his judgment; and failure brought no humiliation. It cannot be denied that he attached too much importance to hostile criticism, for he never perceived his own weight; but the appreciation of his superiors reconciled him to any annoyance.

General Harcourt's letter marks the time when he began to give his attention to the construction of military bridges, on which he afterwards wrote an important work, remarkable for having furnished Rennie and Telford with their first notion of a suspension bridge, as they both avowed. He also designed a pontoon, which was tested by the authorities and reported on favourably, but not brought into use till the following year.

General Jamy retired from the college in December, 1806, and his duties fell on Major Douglas, who soon received the appointment of commandant, with the rank of lieutenant-colonel in the army. He remained at his post through the year, by which time the scientific vein of the army seems to have been exhausted; for in February, 1808, he reports to. the quartermaster-general that so few officers remain in the Senior Department, that he can be spared for active service, and earnestly begs to be employed in an expedition then known to be fitting out.

He refers to the manner in which he has been shut out from service, when it opened the road to honour, and hopes that he may not be compelled to show his desire for it by "a great sacrifice,"—the resignation of his post at the college. General Brownrigg's answer was all he could wish:—

> If I should be so fortunate as to succeed in an earnest request, I have made to be employed in my present staff situation (in the expedition on foot), I shall consider myself proud to have the advantage of your talents and experience. I have not failed to communicate your wishes to the commander-in-chief, who expressed much satisfaction at the perusal of your letter.

He was now to have a respite from study in the dangers of the field, but not before he had turned out the men who were to be the lieutenants of Wellington, and who won for him the testimony which the duke so characteristically expressed—"Douglas is a d——d clever fellow!"

CHAPTER 11

With Sir John Moore

Colonel Douglas had been deeply interested by the conflict raging in Spain, and his feelings were those of every Englishman in every grade of society. The national sympathy could not be withheld from a people struggling for their country trepanned by a foreign despot, and overrun by his armies; but something more seemed claimed when the invader was the common enemy. The same power had threatened England with the same ruin, and the wounds of Spain might tomorrow be our own, whence a desire arose to support the Spaniards with a military force. This led to the despatch of an expedition under Lieutenant-General Sir John Moore, a host in himself, but who could do little execution with a handful of soldiers.

Colonel Douglas was appointed Assistant Quartermaster-General to the expedition in the autumn of 1808, and ordered to set out with despatches for Sir John Moore. The telegraph directed the admiral commanding at Plymouth to hold a vessel ready for the service, and he hired and equipped a small cutter, being unable to spare a man-of-war. Colonel Douglas arrived the next day, and proceeded to sea as soon as they obtained a wind, though it blew hard, and the sky threatened bad weather.

A strong easterly gale swept the Bay of Biscay, and the cutter rolled along under close-reefed trysail with the main boom lodged and bowsprit run in, waves bursting over the deck, and keeping it almost under water during the whole voyage, though the captain managed the little craft very cleverly. Colonel Douglas bore the tossing for a week, when he began to think they must be near Vigo, and found the distance had been run by log, though there was no appearance of a port. It now transpired that the captain's navigation was less perfect than his seamanship; for he had set out for Spain without a chart of the coast, though he had never been there, and nothing remained but to stay at sea till they could inquire their way. The weather was thick, the rolling what it always is in that quarter, and their position only guessed.

Colonel Douglas recommended that they should heave to, and the captain agreed, but had not time to carry out his intention, for a cry rose of "A sail to starboard," and another and another followed till they sighted a whole fleet. This proved to be British transports in charge of a frigate, and came on under all sail. The cutter bore away for the man-of-war, making a signal which brought her to, and the skipper revealed his difficulty in coming round, asking for information. His inquiry infuriated the captain of His Majesty's ship *Diana*, thus pulled up to tell a cutter the way to Vigo, and he answered wide, referring him to a region of objectionable repute. But the announcement that the cutter had an officer on board with despatches for Sir John Moore made all right, and he directed the cutter to fall in with the fleet, as they were bound for Vigo, and she had only to follow the frigate's lead. They all anchored in Vigo Bay the same evening.

The French had scattered the Spanish Armies, but this had not deterred Sir John Moore from pushing forward, though the enemy mustered three hundred thousand men, and the English numbered only twenty-five thousand. A cavalry action was fought on the 15th of December, when the English hussars defeated a greatly superior force; though sometimes obliged to dismount and lead their horses, in consequence of the ice and snow on the ground.

Sir John Moore continued his operations, and made arrangements for a general attack; but Napoleon hastened up with an overwhelming force, which compelled him to retire.

Colonel Douglas met the retreating army at Benevente, at the moment held by the English cavalry, with parties guarding the fords of the Esla, which the infantry had crossed. But six hundred sabres of the French Imperial Guard succeeded in dashing over the river, and drove back the videttes, when they encountered Lieutenant-General Lord Paget, who held them in check till reinforced by a detachment of the 10th Hussars. The combat then became furious, and seemed doubtful for a time, but ended in the repulse of the French, who fled across the river, after a heavy loss of killed, wounded and prisoners.

Colonel Douglas could have been in no position more fruitful of experience than the one he now held; for his duties connected him with every arrangement, and all his energies were called out by the destitution of the army. The retreat was one of the severest ever imposed on British soldiers, and is only surpassed by the flight of the French from Moscow. Officers and men endured the same privations, hurrying through a ravaged country without food and in ragged clothing, exposed to the most rigorous weather, and incessant attacks from the enemy. The roads were deep with snow, which continued to fall, and many sunk to their knees in the ruts, where their boots were torn off, leaving them to march on barefoot. Colonel Douglas exerted himself to alleviate these privations, and with such success that the quartermaster-general's department issued new blankets and a hundred and fifty pairs of shoes to every regiment two days after he joined the army, in the midst of the retreat.

It would be out of the province of this book to follow the steps of the troops, but it may be mentioned that they kept Colonel Douglas in the saddle day and night, while his duties brought him to every threatened point, so that he witnessed the charges of the French cavalry, the drunken scene at Bembibia, and the entanglement with the broken army of Romana. The French held the rear-guard in a constant skirmish, and it was thus engaged when the bullocks drawing the treasure fell down, blocking the road with the waggons, and he now saw the adroitness with which Sir John Moore met difficulties. The road could only be cleared by emptying the waggons, and leaving their load behind; but this might lead to a scramble and endanger the safety of the rear-guard.

The general avoided such a catastrophe by having the casks of dollars rolled to the side of the road, and there tumbled over a precipice. The light company of the 28th stood by with orders to shoot anyone who left the ranks, but not a man stirred. No restraint was placed on the camp-followers, and they could not resist the attraction of the coin, which burst from the casks as they split against the rocks, and invited them to risk knee and neck in the pursuit. A few waifs on the road detained the French when they came up, securing a little breathing-time to the English rear-guard. But Soult continued to press on, and thus forced the Battle of Corunna, which taught him the superiority of English troops, though at the cost of their general's life.

Colonel Douglas was in another part of the field at the moment that Sir John Moore thus fell, shattered by a cannon-ball; and his duties prevented him joining the little train which carried the body to the ramparts, though he saw it borne away as the dirge narrates. A later incident of his life connects him with the story, and forms its sequel, now related for the first time. After recording the hero's death, Napier says:

The guns of the enemy paid him funeral honours, and Soult, with a noble feeling of respect for his valour, raised a monument to his memory. (*Peninsular War,* vol. 1.)

Sir Howard Douglas has left a note disproving this statement. The monument was not erected by Soult, but by the Marquis de Romana, who returned to Corunna at the head of a Spanish Army on its evacuation by the French, when they advanced into Portugal. The gallant Spaniard saw the unmarked grave, and placed over it a memorial of timber, painted to imitate stone, and representing the broken shaft of a column, rising from a pediment, with trophies formed of real guns and shells. He repaired to the spot in state on the completion of the structure, attended by his staff, the civil authorities of the town, and the garrison, while the whole population lined the way, and the solemnity was heightened by the mournful strains of bands of music. The marquis uncovered the monument in presence of this assembly, and wrote on it the following inscription in black chalk, with his own hand:—

A la gloria del Excellentissimo Señor
Don Juan Moore,
General en gefe del Exercitos Britannicos,
Y a la de sus valientes soldados.
La Espagnia Agradecida
Battaglia do Elvina: Januario 16 de 1809.

Spain has been reproached with ingratitude to England, but gratitude never looked nobler than in this incident.

A description of the memorial was forwarded to the prince regent by Major-General Sir Robert Walker, and Colonel Douglas was ordered by the Minister for War to convert it into a permanent structure, on his being employed in Spain a second time. He was to carry out the work by fitting the compartments with slabs of marble, which were to bear a Latin inscription furnished by Dr. Parr.

But the proposed change of inscription struck him as injudicious, and he suggested that nothing could equal what had been written on the monument by Romana, and urged that it should be retained. Government adopted his counsel, and he had the satisfaction of completing the work, thus paying the last duty to his commander. (The author has no doubt these facts ultimately became known to his lamented friend Sir William Napier, who must have heard them from Sir Howard's own lips.)

Errors have also crept into the reports of the embarkation, and not unaccountably, for it was chiefly effected at night. The baggage had been embarked on the 13th, under the superintendence of Colonel Douglas and his department; and their excellent arrangements now prevented confusion as the troops, artillery, and ambulances poured in a stream through the streets, lit by the fire of the picquets. The movement was covered by the rear-guard, which held the land-fronts of the fortifications across the isthmus, facing the enemy, who watched for the moment when these should be evacuated, leaving the rear-guard at his mercy. Colonel Douglas saw the danger, and resolved to make an effort to ward it off.

His duties brought him in contact with the Spanish authorities, and he made them see that Corunna would be treated as captured by assault if the enemy found the works undefended on the retirement of the English, while they might now be taken over by the relics of Romana's army, and held long enough to cover the embarkation of the rear-guard and command terms for themselves, though they were not equal to standing a regular siege. His suggestions were communicated to the Spanish general, and that officer despatched a message to General Hill, requesting possession of the works, and pledging his honour to hold them till all the English had embarked.

The arrangement was carried out, but not unnoted by the French, who brought up their field-guns and opened fire on the transports. The terrors of the scene were heightened by night. The admiral signalled for the transports to make off, and more than a hundred slipped their cables, running before the wind out of the bay, and heaving to in the offing, while the rear-guard mustered on the beach within the citadel.

A number of the transports ran foul of each other, entangling their rigging; and several were wrecked, but their crews got off in boats, after setting the ships on fire. A naval officer called from a boat to Colonel Douglas, and said he was told by the admiral to look out for him and take him on board the *Barfleur*.

But he waited to watch the embarkation of the rear-guard, as it threatened to be hazardous—the transports being only accessible by a long pull to seaward; and casualties might have occurred if Sir Samuel Hood had not sent all his boats to bring the troops to the *Barfleur* and *Resolution*, lying near the shore, and which he turned into receiving-ships. Colonel Douglas ascribes their preservation to this arrangement, claiming no credit for himself; though he must have felt conscious of some share in the achievement when he thus summed it up in his notes:

All being taken off, those two ships got under way, and with great coolness and no hurry moved majestically down to the fleet to leeward.

CHAPTER 12

At Walcheren

The dockyards and arsenals of England again rang with preparation; pressgangs were busy; vessels were taken up as transports; and regiments ordered to hold themselves in readiness for embarkation. It became known that government was equipping an armament for another little blow at the enemy; and the Horse Guards was flooded with applications for employment. Repeated disasters had not checked the expectations of statesmen or the confidence of the public, and they once more dreamt of success, blind to the fact that petty expeditions are a waste of power, and can never achieve an object worth a war.

The death of his half-brother, Sir William, raised Colonel Douglas to the baronetcy, as he was afforded this opening for further service. He had now every inducement to remain at home, if his ambition could be satisfied with hereditary rank, a lucrative post, and an honourable position, not to mention his sympathies as a husband and father, whose life was invaluable to a young family. Nor could he expect that the expedition on foot would prove equal to the object in view, for it sought nothing less than the forcing of the Western Scheldt, and the destruction of the enemy's resources at Antwerp; and these results could not be achieved by a few thousand soldiers.

But such considerations failed to shake his purpose, and he again applied for employment. General Brownrigg invited him to join the assembling force as assistant quartermaster-general, his old post; and he readily agreed. Lady Douglas gave her consent with tears. "I was old-fashioned enough to ask it," he writes to General Harcourt; but the mention of her tears is all that he betrays of her objections.

The expedition mustered in the Downs on the 27th of July. Great attention had been paid to its equipment, which included six of the military bridges invented by Sir Howard and constructed at Woolwich.

★★★★★★

"We received orders last night to construct six of your military bridges, and one or two carts to carry them. We are, however, making three (carts). There has nothing in the way of alteration occurred to me worth telling."—Letter from Lieut.-Colonel Millar, R.A., to Sir Howard Douglas, in the *Douglas Papers*.

★★★★★★

Sir Howard embarked with Lord Chatham, the general commanding-in-chief, and his staff, in the *Venerable* line-of-battle ship, bearing the flag of the admiral, Sir Richard Strachan. Sail was made next morning at five o'clock, and the ship came to anchor in the Stone Deep, off Walcheren, at seven in the evening. Here she was joined by other ships of the fleet bringing the left wing of the army under Lieutenant-General Sir John Hope, while a squadron under Commodore Owen proceeded to Weeling Passage with the division of Lieutenant-General the Marquis of Huntley.

It had originally been intended to make a rush at Antwerp from the coast of Flanders; but such an enterprise would cut the army off from the fleet, and naval co-operation was considered indispensable: so government diverted the attack to a point where ships could act, and the troops were accompanied by a squadron and flotilla, which promised a support, while it secured transport for the equipment. The breakdown in this service foiled every operation on shore.

After vacillating between several projects, Lord Chatham decided on a plan of attack combining three operations—namely: a disembarkation on the island of Walcheren; the occupation of the islands of North and South Beveland; and the reduction of some strong batteries commanding the entrance to the West Scheldt on the island of Cadsand, which was to be carried out by the division of Lieutenant-General the Marquis of Huntley. The left wing effected a landing on Walcheren the same evening, and the reserve occupied the Bevelands early on the following day, the 1st of August; but the troops could not be disembarked at Cadsand, owing to the tempestuous weather. Thus, the miscarriages of the expedition began at the beginning.

Sir Howard Douglas was charged with the departmental arrangements of the first brigade, which landed under the command of Lieutenant-General Sir Eyre Coote; but was accompanied by the whole headquarter staff, as well as Lord Chatham. They got ashore without damage, though the enemy fired from Den Haak Fort at the covering vessels, and made an attempt to dispute a small wood which the light troops advanced to secure. But they then abandoned Den Haak Fort, and Lord Chatham fixed his headquarters there, while Colonel Pack hurried forward to seize the town of Terr Verr. Heavy firing came from this direction in the evening, exciting fears for the safety of his small force; and Sir Howard Douglas was despatched to ascertain its position. He reached the spot about eleven at night, and discovered Colonel Pack close to Verr, with four companies of the 71st.

The little band had advanced in face of a strong corps, but met such a hot reception that they fell back, leaving a number of dead. Sir Howard galloped back to Den Haak Fort, after he had seen them reinforced by Major-General Clinton, with the 50th Regiment; and there found Rear-Admiral Sir Home Popham, who heard his report, and settled with the commander-in-chief to take up the gunboats. These made their way to the town by the Veer Gat, under the command of Sir Home himself, while Sir Howard returned to the land force, which had been strengthened in the meantime, and concerted measures for a combined attack. The gunboats opened fire at seven in the morning, and the troops completed the investment by eight; but the garrison made a stout resistance, inflicting heavy loss before they surrendered: nor could the gunboats prevent more than two hundred getting off by water, and entering Flushing.

Sir Howard now joined the force detailed to attack Ramakins, and was present at the surrender of that post, which left the gunboats free to complete the investment of Flushing. Lord Chatham had been struck by his acquaintance with naval movements, and now selected him as his medium of communication with the admiral—a delicate trust, owing to the jealousy with which the two commanders regarded each other. Nor could all his tact impart animation to Sir Richard Strachan, who held back the flotilla and thus delayed the investment.

Precious days were lost when moments told, and the town retained its communications by water, which admitted succours and supplies. Nothing could be more fatal to the object of the expedition, which was only attainable by a dash; for the pause enabled the French to advance their forces, and place Antwerp out of danger. Nor did its evils end here; for the baneful air of the swamps engendered fever—more destructive than the sword—and the English fell before it in files.

Sir Howard retained his fortitude through this misery, and never suffered his misgivings to appear. His duties kept him employed, and made his talent apparent to everyone, whence he was pronounced one of the ablest officers of the army by Sir John Macleod, who commanded the artillery at the siege. (This is stated on the authority of General Sir Robert Gardiner, G.C.B., the son-in-law of Sir John Macleod.) His kindness to the sick and wounded is remembered after half a century, and cost him some sacrifice; for he denied himself indulgences that he might minister to their wants. He obtained the confidence of both the general and admiral, who agreed here, when every other point found them differ; and this led to his being named in orders as the staff officer appointed to decide the moment when the fleet should open fire on the final assault of the town.

The post assigned him was the Nolle battery, directed against the sea-line of the enemy's works, which commanded the entrance to the West Scheldt, and could only be passed safely under cover. Hence his orders left him a discretionary power as to the time when he should call for the fire of the squadron; but he signalled the admiral that all was ready as soon as the officer in charge of the siege-batteries made his report. The ships instantly weighed, and seven sail-of-the-line had come within the enemy's range, where shot were beginning to strike their hulls and rigging, before he gave the signal to fire. This was the discharge of the second gun from the Nolle battery, on which the fleet poured forth its broadsides, and the other guns of the battery opened on the sea-line works at the same moment, firing with such precision as to disable the guns commanding the passage.

Thus, he covered the advance of the fleet by carrying out his own principle of massing an overpowering force on the vital point. He remained so cool amidst the action, that he employed himself in watching the ricocheting of the enemy's shot along the surface of the sea, and his notes describe it as:

An admirable opportunity of observing the great value and importance of that description of practice in naval warfare.

Sea and land joined in the bombardment, encircling Flushing with fire, while shells and rockets tore through the air; and the kind soldier was touched with pity as he saw a town in flames. He joyfully obeyed an order from Lord Chatham to suspend firing. The commander-in-chief had resolved to demand a surrender, and an officer was despatched to General Monnet, requiring the French to give up the town and yield themselves prisoners of war. But an hour and a half elapsed without bringing a definite answer, and the English resumed the bombardment; nor did the enemy accept the invitation to capitulate till the afternoon of the next day. The firing then ceased, and the garrison surrendered.

Sir Howard improved the "admirable opportunity" of the bombardment to mark its results in every particular. The pressure of his departmental duties left him no unoccupied time, but he rose an hour earlier, in the morning, that he might go round the seawall at low water, and examine the effect produced by the fire of the line-of-battle ships. The wall had been penetrated by some of the shot, and others were sticking in the face, but there was no breach, and the greatest number of shot were lying on the beach. The embrasures had received a battering, as had the crests of the parapets, and shot had dismounted guns and broken their carriages, while those which passed, over had riddled the neighbouring houses and knocked down a little brickwork.

But he found that it was the land batteries, and the rockets and shells, which had produced the greatest impression on the town, setting it on fire at several points, and reducing one quarter to a ruin. This led him to conclusions which we shall see him urging when fleets were used in bombardments during the late war with Russia, and his notes express a conviction that Flushing could not have been taken without the operations on land.

The capture proved of no importance, for the time had gone by for an attack on Antwerp, which now possessed a garrison of 20,000 men, while the fortifications had been strengthened, and the passage of the river barred by twelve line-of-battle ships. Approach by land was cut off by the breaching of the dykes, which inundated the surrounding country, and every assailable point had its fort and garrison. But the British squadron was not commanded by Nelson, and no defences were necessary against an army smitten by pestilence, and perishing where it stood. General Brownrigg reports the sick at 3,000 on Saturday, the 26th of August; the Monday found it 4,000; and a few days raised it to 7,000. Then a Council of War decided on returning to England, while there were still troops to re-embark.

So disastrous a failure excited a general outcry. It seemed a repetition of the blunders in Holland on a larger scale, and parties united against a system which employed such commanders. The bitterest harangues were directed against the government; Parliament ordered an inquiry into the conduct of the expedition; and newspapers mingled satire with invective in criticising the operations. The friends of the two commanders heightened the agitation by their bitter recriminations: one side maintained that the general had behaved with skill, but was foiled by the inaction of the admiral; while the party of Sir Richard Strachan contended that he would have captured Antwerp, had he not been held back by Lord Chatham. Hence arose the well-known epigram:—

> *The Earl of Chatham, with his sword drawn,*
> *Stood waiting for Sir Richard Strachan:*
> *Sir Richard, longing to be at 'em,*
> *Stood waiting for the Earl of Chatham.*

Sir Howard returned to his duties at the Military College, and took no part in the controversy, but Lord Chatham and General Brownrigg claimed his assistance in their defence. A memorandum in the *Douglas Papers* shows that he gave his testimony to the authorities in favour of Lord Chatham, ascribing the detention at Walcheren to the imperfect co-operation of the naval force, though he expresses doubts whether any combination of the two commanders would have achieved the design on Antwerp. The methodical way in which he had jotted down the points of the campaign now proved of service, by showing the occasions on which naval co-operation failed; and the following letters attest the importance attached to the journal prepared from these notes for the vindication of Lord Chatham.

Horse Guards,
20th September, 1809.

My dear Sir Howard,

I had hoped for the pleasure of hearing of, or seeing something of you before this time, and trust I shall not be much longer disappointed. The clamour that has been raised against Lord Chatham, and the extraordinary state in which the government of the country is, make it more than ever necessary that the most comprehensive and satisfactory statement of the transactions of the army he commanded should be made, and that with the least possible loss of time. As you have commenced this work, I hope to have your able assistance in completing it. I think this might be done if you could spare a week or ten days in town; and if Lady Douglas will accompany you, it will afford my daughter and myself the greatest pleasure to endeavour to make your time pass pleasantly, and we would try to get you lodgings near us. Pray let me hear from you on this subject, and believe me

Truly and faithfully yours,   Robert Brownrigg.

Horse Guards,
28th September, i809

My dear Sir Howard,

On coming to the office, I found a note from Colonel Taylor, expressing the king's anxiety to receive Lord Chatham's report as early as possible. This I shall communicate to Lord C. in the morning, and I have no doubt that His Lordship will press for the *Journal*. I only mention this to request your attention to the completion of it; and to suggest that possibly you may postpone your journey to Lord Harcourt until this business is finished, that you may devote your undivided time to it. I shall certainly hope to meet you here on Monday.

Ever truly yours,

Robert Brownrigg.

The *Journal* was ordered to be printed and laid before Parliament. It details the operations day by day, and mentions the officers employed in a prominent manner, with the exception of Sir Howard himself, whom we can only trace under the modest designation of "an officer of the quartermaster-general's department."

CHAPTER 13

In Galicia

Sir Howard's experience of war had not cooled his military ardour. In his quiet sphere at the college he gave his thoughts to the conflicts waged abroad, where glory waited on danger. From every camp he received letters from his pupils, relating what passed, as well as what was in prospect; and their plain unvarnished narratives made him impatient of inaction. But it was the struggle in Spain that he watched most earnestly: his Spanish campaign had interested him in its people, and excited a desire to serve under Lord Wellington, an object he would gladly have purchased by the sacrifice of his position at home.

Unknown to himself events were working to bring about his wishes, though in a way he could never have conceived, and which left his position untouched. The minister of the day had heard of the officer who came to the rescue of his superiors on the Walcheren inquiry, and now thought of him for another delicate service, calling for the same tact. The first hint came to Sir Howard in the following note from Colonel Torrens, the Military Secretary:—

> Horse Guards,
> July 24th, 1811
>
> My dear Douglas,
> Immediately on the receipt of this, the Duke (of York) requests that you will come to town. In order that you and Lady Douglas may be prepared for what is to happen, I beg to apprise you that it is intended to send you upon a confidential and important mission to Spain.
> Yours ever sincerely,
> H. Torrens.

Six days later he heard from the Minister for War, in an official communication from Downing Street, and learnt that:

> It being judged expedient, under present circumstances, that an officer of the British Army should be appointed to reside in the province of Galicia, for the purpose of communicating with the commanders of the Spanish Armies in that and the adjoining provinces of Spain, and of distributing such arms and stores as may be sent from this country, His Royal Highness the Prince Regent has directed that you should be selected for this service.

The letter enjoined him "to lose no time in repairing to the headquarters of Lieutenant-General Lord Wellington, Commander-in-Chief of the British Forces in the Peninsula," and placing himself under his orders; while he received instructions to keep in communication with Lord Liverpool, and forward him copies of all his letters to Lord Wellington for the information of the prince regent.

Sir Howard did not neglect the admonition to "lose no time;" for he set out for Plymouth the next day, after a long interview with Lord Wellesley. His coming was awaited by a man-of-war schooner, appropriately named the *Active*, and she started, on her voyage directly he stepped on board. For once he got a fair wind, and the *Active* reached the Tagus on the 12th of August, ten days after she had left England.

The voyager nowhere meets a pleasanter surprise than in this river, where he passes from a bay of storms into smooth water, almost in a breath, changing the cliffs for green slopes flanked by vineyards and windmills. But the scene now excited a feeling of sadness, for Sir Howard could not forget the presence of war, which had made the rest of the country a desert, and he reflected that all might have been as fair and smiling but for this irruption. He became impatient to join Lord Wellington, and the admiral's boat met them near the bar, which enabled him to go rapidly up the river, and he reached Lisbon before the evening.

Here there was nothing to mark the situation but swarms of beggars, infesting the streets, and betraying the ruin of the population; for the Tagus caught an air of bustle from the squadron in the basin and a crowd of transports, and the city wore its best dress in honour of the regent's birthday. The houses streamed with flags, and the great square offered the attraction of a parade of Portuguese troops, who were firing a salute as Sir Howard arrived. Night brought an illumination, which he found of great use in picking his steps through the city, a pit of darkness, and noted for its abominations. "Edinburgh is nothing to it," he writes to Lady Douglas.

He had wished to set off for the quarters of the army, but this he was obliged to forego, having important business with the quarter-master-general, who could not be seen till next day; and he would have experienced difficulty in escaping from a party of roisterers, who caught him up as he was looking about, and carried him off to dinner. The names of these choice spirits are not revealed, but a suspicion arises that the dinner must have been at the expense of the regent, as they evinced an exuberant appreciation of His Royal Highness, first drinking his health in sherry, then in champagne, and then in claret, finishing with what Sir Howard marks by *et cetera*. But potations pottle-deep offered no seduction to one habitually temperate, and it is a proof of his sobriety on the occasion that he went from the dinner to the theatre, and brought away a notion of the performance for Lady Douglas.

His business in Lisbon was despatched next morning, and he started post for headquarters, which the retreat of Soult and Marmont had advanced to the frontier. His arrival found Lord Wellington absent; but he saw him on his return, and Sir Howard drew a favourable augury from his simple manners. The Great Captain read the instructions from Lord Liverpool, "made some short, clear, and striking observations on the state of the war as regarded Galicia," (letter from Sir Howard to Lady Douglas), and described his present position, which he had taken up to protect that province, while he threatened Ciudad Rodrigo. He threw off his reserve as he penetrated Sir Howard's character, and condescended to explain his objects, instead of simply giving orders.

He declared his intention of besieging Ciudad Rodrigo as soon as the enemy's movements should leave him to carry on the operation without interruption; but he remarked that even the fall of that place would not free the army for other service until the Spanish authorities could undertake the defence of Galicia. Hence it was of the utmost importance that Sir Howard should exert himself to place them in this position, which could only be done by reorganising the broken Galician Army, and employing it to draw attention from the British commander. Sir Howard dined with Lord Wellington in the evening, and learnt that an appointment on the general staff had been given to his cousin, Captain Charles Douglas, in order that he might accompany him as *aide-de-camp*, the rank held by Sir Howard not entitling him to such an attendant.

With the morning's light the two kinsmen were mounted, and galloped off to the cantonments of the Horse Artillery, where they stopped to breakfast with an old comrade. They made another halt at Fuentes d'Onores, and Sir Howard received an account of the fight, as Charles Douglas led him from point to point of the fields, showing the positions in which he had been engaged for three days with the enemy. Relics of the battle still littered the ground, and they passed mournfully by the graves of the dead, buried where they fell, friend and foe in the same pit.

Another day's journey brought them to Almeida, where they were surprised with a good dinner, to which they were invited by George Macleod. of the Engineers; and the same friend gave them breakfast in the morning, starting them on their way. They would have fared badly but for this hospitality, as the town was in ruins, and the surrounding district had been left by the French as if swept by Attila. Everywhere they met the same devastation, compelling them to carry necessaries for themselves; and they were obliged to keep a constant watch against the peasants, who eased them of little traps at every stage.

This made the journey more harassing, and it was a great relief to embark on the Douro, where a boat had been provided for their reception. They rapidly descended the river, and might forget the misery they had witnessed amidst the scenery on either side, blending rock and mountain and forest with castle and monastery, perched where foot could scarcely climb. But it is difficult to enjoy the picturesque in a dirty boat which is half full of water, and smells not the sweetest, so that they felt little disposition to loiter.

An autumn evening induced them to land at a rural mansion, which looked a paradise from the river, and raised a hope of comfortable quarters. But appearances proved deceptive; for its master had fled on the advance of the French, and left behind a garrison of fleas, which held possession against all comers. They exceeded the audacity of the rats at Tynemouth Castle, and Sir Howard spent the night in striking lights and making charges, while his cousin and servant were employed in the same manner. Nor were their miseries confined to discomfort; for the servant went to bed leaving his door unlocked, and arose in the morning to find himself bereft of everything but the equipment in which he had lain down. He rubbed his eyes as he looked round for his coat, breeches, and other invaluables, and could hardly believe that they were missing, till it flashed across him that the fleas had carried them off.

Sir Howard writes to Lady Douglas:

Poor fellow! his look when he came to tell me of it set me screaming with laughter. I must refit him entirely.

A couple of hours in the morning brought them to Oporto, and Sir Howard was occupied for the remainder of the day with the authorities, though he found time to inspect the bridge and fortifications. Indeed, he observed the military features of the country all through his journey, marking and sketching the positions, ascertaining the capabilities of the defensive works of the various towns, and noting where rivers could be forded, and roads commanded by boats. Nor did he forget the loved circle of his home, turning to it in this ride of nine hundred miles, so taken up with the duties of his mission and his studies as a soldier. He writes to Lady Douglas:

Let my boys read this, and be aware how much I depend on their giving you no cause for uneasiness, but, on the contrary, that they conduct themselves in a manner to be your comfort. Remember, my boys, I depend on this.

So simple and open was his nature, yet so formed to sway others; for what could touch his children like this appeal! His character shows a consistency in these traits when they seem to present a diversity; for they are all truthful and natural. He is the same when "screaming with laughter" at the rueful face of his servant, as when he addresses his children, and draws out their better qualities by his reliance. The good humour is as genial as the good sense, and both are inspired from his heart.

He needed to go but a short distance to learn the condition of Galicia. His first visit to Spain had shown him the noble qualities of its people, and he now came among them more eager for their deliverance. As a race they may repel us at first, but their cold manners disappear on acquaintance, as if they were but a veil over their nature, which is cordial and generous.; They soon bring us to abjure the doctrine that Cervantes lashed chivalry out of Spain. Sir Howard's faith in them was not shaken by their present wretchedness, which had destroyed it in themselves; for Galicia, was differing the horrors of anarchy and military licence combined. The authorities were divided and distracted; the people terror-struck; the army almost naked; the enemy in force on the border, and his way open to Corunna. Hence arose continual panics, rendering the *Junta* powerless; and the city had now reached the last point of misery.

Yet the population were brave and loyal, animated by the noblest spirit, and ready to face the enemy, if they could procure arms and a leader. Such was the posture of affairs when English ships landed a large supply of arms and clothing, which was stored in the town, and rumour announced the arrival of an English officer charged with its distribution and with the organization of resistance. The news brought a crowd to Sir Howard's quarters; guerilla chiefs forced their way to his door; the civil authorities came to pay him their respects; and a feeling grew up that there was yet hope for Galicia.

CHAPTER 14

Doubling up the Enemy

Lord Wellington had warned Sir Howard that his mission would prove full of difficulty. But probably even he was not aware of the obstacles in the way, or the number of interests requiring to be reconciled. The destitution of the Galician Army had compelled it to prey on the country, while it could do nothing for its defence; and hence it became as oppressive as the enemy, and almost as odious. This bad feeling it returned, but more towards the guerillas than the people, as they had increased its discredit by maintaining the resistance it had abandoned. Nor was there less discord among the authorities. No two generals would act in concert; the guerilla chiefs followed their own impulses; the Supreme *Junta* received no obedience from the local ones, and its measures failed to obtain the public confidence.

The disunion was increased by newspapers in French pay, which laboured to excite distrust of England, ascribing her intervention in Spain to a selfish policy, and representing her object to be the acquisition of the Spanish colonies in America, which she sustained in revolt while engaging the Spanish people at home. Such assertions made a deep impression on a nation jealous of foreigners, and this became so apparent that Lord Wellington advised Mr. Wellesley to hire one or two newspapers to rebut the attacks. He wrote:

> This is a matter, however, to be managed with great secrecy and discretion, and whatever you should think proper to publish should be confined to a simple statement of facts and dates, in plain language, with the obvious reasoning resulting from them. (Wellington Despatches.)

The course taken by Sir Howard accorded with this counsel—all his dealings with the Galician authorities and people being frank and truthful. It came to be known that he meant what he said, that he spoke only the truth, and that he would never waver from what he had stated. They saw that he persisted in following out his objects through every difficulty, and could neither be turned aside by opposition, nor misled by deception; for he succeeded through his energy on the one hand, and established such a system of intelligence that he was rarely matched on the other.

At the same time, his character inspired respect as well as confidence—for the one fell to his talent and activity, the other to his address and zeal, his kind and winning manners, and his appreciation of the national capabilities, so soothing to the proud spirits with which he came in contact. Thus a few weeks raised him to authority, and his influence spread so far that messengers came from the Pyrenees for his counsel and assistance.

One of his first acts was to visit the hospitals, where he found the sick without blankets, and he issued a supply the same day from the stores at his disposal. Soon afterwards he heard of a wounded Frenchman, in a hospital out of the town, and went to pay him a visit, when he discovered that the Spanish officials had neglected to give out the blankets, and he made arrangements for their distribution on the spot. He also sent a convoy of clothing to the Spanish Army, and furnished the guerilla bands of Longa and Minas with 300 carbines and 1200 muskets. (Despatch to general Lord Wellington.)

He remained some weeks at Corunna to carry out his measures, and then proceeded to join the army of General Abadia, who had fixed his headquarters at Ponperada. Manifestations of goodwill met him at every step, and attested the impression he had made. Passengers raised their hats as he passed, the postmasters refused payment for their horses, and the Marquis Porlasga rode out to invite him to a banquet, on hearing that he was near his mansion. A report of his approach reached the camp, and General Abadia and the chief of his Staff hastened to pay him their respects. The following day he arrived at headquarters, and received visits from General Castaños and the chiefs of corps and departments, who all showed him the utmost respect and consideration.

Next morning, he reviewed the army, and found it in a worse condition than he had expected, half the soldiers being without trowsers, and wearing only *capots*, while the clothing of the rest showed great room for improvement. But they were a fine body of men, standing well, though deeply marked by privation, and as badly trained as equipped. The best corps only manoeuvred singly, not attempting movements of the line, and a Toledo battalion broke down in trying to change front in *échelon*. The cavalry were on a level with the infantry, and moved with wide gaps between the squadrons, nor could they go accurately through the sword exercise. Their horses might all be thought to have come from La Mancha, each being a Rosinante; and the artillery was as wretchedly manned as horsed.

The muster did not correspond with the reported numbers, which led Sir Howard to make inquiries, and he learnt that nearly half the army was employed by the officers as cooks and servants. It became his duty to urge General Abadia both to correct this abuse and to raise the quality of the troops by having them drilled. This was touching points very irritating to a jealous commander, but he contrived to avoid offence, though he did not attain his object—General Abadia pleading the sanction of custom for the number of servants. Sir Howard represented that the country now called for every man in the field, and entreated him to allow no custom to stand in the way; and he then consented to open the subject to General Castaños.

The drill was more easily settled, as his strictures could not be denied, and the general pledged himself to give it attention. His suggestions were not taken so kindly by the officers of the army, and the good feeling he had elicited disappeared when they became aware that he had attacked their privileges. They showed their resentment on the first opportunity, which arose on an order from General Abadia to send round the order-book to the English commissioner, according to the custom of regular armies; and the chief of the staff announced that the staff would make a remonstrance if the order were not withdrawn. Such was the notion entertained of the relations of officers to their commander! General Abadia yielded the point, bat warded off the affront by arranging that Sir Howard should receive his private order-book.

Sir Howard made allowance for the irritation of a defeated army, suspicions of interference, and took no umbrage—not being obliged to see what had occurred, and thinking it a moment to evince goodwill. He wished to raise the pride of the troops, believing that proper training would endue them with high qualities; and he seized every occasion of expressing this opinion, and acquiring their confidence. He made way from the first, and gradually the feeling against him subsided, as all recognised his zeal and diligence, his interest in the soldiers, attention to the sick, and unfailing suavity and courtesy.

Yet he worked on delicate ground; for General Abadia failed in his promise to improve the drill of the troops, and they were still untrained in line movements, so that he felt obliged to renew the pressure. It required continued efforts to set the general in motion, and the absence of energy affected the soldiers, who made little progress, though a change appeared after a few weeks, and gave them the look of an army. He also succeeded in reducing the number of servants, which increased the effective force by four thousand men.

The object he had first in view was now attained. The troops were in a condition to march; and he reported the fact to Lord Wellington, though apprehending difficulty with General Abadia. And the result transcended his fears, for the general proved immovable. Sir Howard represented the importance of an advance, both as a support to the operations of Lord Wellington, and a means of gaining the public confidence, while he affirmed that it would have the best effect on the army itself. But the general maintained that there was no cohesion in the army, and no subsistence in its front—alleging one excuse upon another as the commissioner parried his objections. Nor could it be denied that the march would be attended with difficulty, but Sir Howard asserted that obstacles would always exist, while an advance could not often be made with the same effect; and he pointed out to the general the honour he would acquire by embracing the opportunity.

The general broke in with an exclamation, assigning the task to his successor, and drew forth a letter he had prepared for the Supreme *Junta*, in which he accused them of having rendered him powerless by leaving him without resources, and declared that he had resolved to strip off his uniform if they did not sanction his retirement, and leave the army where it stood, as he could not retain the command with honour, and honour was dearer to him than life. This disclosure stunned Sir Howard, as it dashed his hopes of a movement at the moment that he looked for their fulfilment, bringing all his projects to the ground. He writes in a memorandum-book which he seems to have carried about:

What could I say to the chief who intended to desert his country's cause?

It was nothing that the general was incompetent for his position; his retirement would create a panic, and he must be persuaded to remain at all hazards. Sir Howard begged him to consider whether the government had not failed him through want of means—not of will; and stated his conviction that honour bound him to his post, be the conduct of the government what it might, nor would he stand acquitted before the country if he took any other course.

This brief note gives but a glimpse of the interview, for he remarks that it did not call for record, as the impression it made upon him could never be effaced. And we may understand his agitation if we picture to ourselves the Spaniard detailing his grievances in a burst of frenzy, and remember the gravity of the crisis, the point in debate, and the consequences hinging on the issue. He must have weighed every word as he interposed, from a fear of using some argument which might have the opposite effect from what he intended; and he may then have thought it well to leave him to reflection, for he retired without asking his decision.

They met again in a day or two, when the Spanish commander was still out of humour, but did not refer to their conference, and Sir Howard renewed his proposal that the army should make a movement. He received an evasive reply, but found the general had no intention of advancing, and had actually sent off his best regiments to join an expedition fitting out at Cadiz for the reconquest of the colonies. It seems incredible that a government should attempt such an enterprise when unable to defend its own soil; but the finest battalions of Spain were now swept off for this service, and it absorbed munitions that would have delivered a blow at home.

Sir Howard heard of the expedition just as he received an application for supplies, and declared that he would give nothing more, except for the equipment of troops brought immediately into the field. But General Abadia no longer concealed his design of remaining inactive, and informed him that he had apprised General Castaños of his intention to retreat to Lugo, as he could not hold his present ground for want of provisions. His letter reached Sir Howard simultaneously with one from Lord Wellington, stating that he had opened his trenches before Ciudad Rodrigo, and that the French would probably muster their whole force to interrupt his operations, whence he begged that they might be kept employed in Galicia by the Spanish Army.

★★★★★★

The following is Earl Wellington's despatch to Sir Howard on this occasion:—

Gallegos, Jan. 10th, 1812.

I request you to inform General Abadia that I am now engaged in the siege of Ciudad Rodrigo, which we are carrying on with the greatest activity. We broke ground before the place on the 8th at night, within 600 yards, having carried a redoubt by storm on that evening at that distance. We shall open our fire, I hope, on the 13th, from the first parallel.

It would be very desirable if General Abadia would endeavour to make some movement to draw the attention of the enemy from us, as I think it probable that they will collect their whole force to endeavour to interrupt our operations.

Ever, dear Sir, yours most faithfully,

Wellington,

Lieut.-Colonel Sir Howard Douglas, Bart.

★★★★★★

Sir Howard determined not to leave his chief without support in such a conjuncture, and he addressed a formal letter to General Abadia, representing Lord Wellington's situation, and begging to know what aid he might expect from the Spanish forces. The answer allowed of no misconception; for General Abadia threw the responsibility of his inaction on Sir Howard, since he had refused him supplies.

Such were some of the obstacles which met the commissioner at every step, and so often did he see his efforts frustrated and his plans overthrown. But he was not one to give up his object; and his fertile mind now conceived a measure quite out of his instructions, but which promised the support required. He determined to arm the people.

The law committed the defence of the kingdom to a levy of the masses in the event of invasion, and each district mustered its own band, under the name of an "Alarm." Sir Howard pointed out to the Supreme *Junta* the capabilities of this force, and engaged to equip it from the English supplies, if the *Junta* would put it on foot. This offer was accepted; arrangements were made for an immediate muster, and the proclamation for a levy appeared within a few days.

The effect surpassed expectation; a patriotic fervour seized all classes, and everyone hastened to the nearest station to enrol himself for service. Sir Howard writes:

Having witnessed with deep regret, the apathy into which the Spanish people had been sinking, on account, among other reasons, of the inefficiency and discomfiture of all their armies, I now beheld with inexpressible satisfaction a fresh outbreak of that popular enthusiasm with which the Galicians first rose on the invaders; and I felt, and still enjoy, the consciousness that I could not be wrong in pursuing a course which rekindled it and inspired them with fresh confidence, calling into new life and vigour that pure national spirit of the Spanish people, to which Great Britain had by acclamation allied herself in their first noble struggle against the French. (Memorandum in the *Douglas Papers*, endorsed "Memo, by Sir Howard on vol. ix. of the Wellington Despatches.")

The proclamation raised the whole country. Sir Howard received the thanks of the *Junta* for his cooperation, and was requested to make a tour of the stations, and inspect the different musters. He set out accordingly, accompanied by the secretary of the *Junta*, and attended by Captain Douglas. Everywhere he met the most touching reception, evincing the gratitude of men, women, and children, who flocked round him in crowds, and hailed him as their deliverer. A brave nation felt itself free, when arms were in every hand.

The muster of the Alarms emboldened the guerillas, whose numbers greatly increased; and the bands of Longa and Minas continually harassed the enemy. Sir Howard had brought the gallantry of these two chiefs to the notice of Lord Liverpool, with a suggestion that it claimed some recognition; and he opportunely received a case of arms, to be presented to them in the name of the British Government. The compliment gratified their pride, and aroused emulation in others; so that hardly a day passed without its conflict, and the enemy could not leave his entrenchments except in force. Hence be could detach no succour to Ciudad Rodrigo without abandoning Asturia; and this required time, though General Bonnet began the operation as soon as he discerned the necessity.

Such a state of affairs infuriated General Abadia, who saw his consequence lessened by the change, and the helm of command taken from his hands. But Sir Howard did not intend to throw him in the background, and now visited his quarters on his old errand, persuaded that a forward movement would defeat the project of Bonnet. General Abadia burst out in exclamations as they met in the presence of his staff, and complained of the proclamation of the *Junta*, as well as the gifts to Longa and Minas.

But he justified both, contending that neither the *Junta* nor himself could have acted differently, as Lord Wellington pressed for support, and that the presents to the guerilla chiefs attested the good feeling of the English Government. He then produced a despatch he had just received from Lord Wellington, again requesting a movement of the army, and convinced him that an advance would retrieve all his credit.

The general agreed to march, but proposed to confine the operation to pushing one line on the Asturias, and another against Astorga, which Sir Howard contended would fail to divert a force from joining Marmont; and he urged a forward movement, as certain to attain this result. Their deliberations were interrupted by the entry of General Mendizabal, and he sided with his chief, maintaining that the Galician Army could not appear in the plain for want of cavalry. The dispute lasted several days, for Sir Howard would not give way, attaching no value to a flank movement, and caring only to employ the army to drive back General Bonnet.

He now obtained intelligence that Bonnet was in motion, while he received from Lord Wellington a more urgent appeal for support, and he prevailed on General Abadia to yield. The Galician Army marched out of its cantonments under a heavy fall of snow, and made its way over execrable roads across the mountains, through streams, in the teeth of a cutting wind, and often knee-deep in drift. The people heard of its advance with joy, the French with wonder, and they fell back as it approached, without venturing a blow. Four days later Sir Howard received the news that Ciudad Rodrigo had fallen.

CHAPTER 15

In Spanish Society

Bonnet now concentrated a force at Astorga, and General Abadia determined to fall back on the great road; to which Sir Howard raised no objection, the purpose of the forward movement being attained. Its success excited joy throughout Galicia, and the English commissioner was hailed with enthusiasm wherever he appeared—for to him the credit was ascribed. None showed him more attention than the clergy and religious orders. He stopped to rest at a convent on his way back from the army, and expressed a wish to pay his respects to the lady abbess, when he was invited to her parlour, and received with the utmost kindness, the abbess insisting on his waiting for a repast. She then conducted him over the convent, and took him to visit the principal sisters in their cells, a favour that had never been granted to a layman before. She gave him her benediction on his departure, and went as far with him towards the door as the rules of her order permitted.

A rumour of his approach reached Santiago, and the Archbishop of Toledo met him outside the city, in a state carriage, and conveyed him to his palace, the population awaiting him in the streets and cheering him to the gates. The archbishop placed the palace at his disposal, and entreated him to consider it his own as long as he remained at Santiago, declaring that he would regard his compliance as an obligation. A chamberlain attended at the door, and marshalled him and his cousin to a noble room, furnished with princely splendour. Here he asked for their orders, and Sir Howard begged for a little tea; for the presence of luxury had no effect on his frugal habits. He thought the chamberlain seemed a little embarrassed by his wish, but imagined that he must be mistaken, when he retired bowing, and a chat with his cousin drove the incident from his mind.

But such an interval passed that the conversation flagged, and they began to think the tea was a long time coming. Their patience met its reward at last; for the chamberlain threw open the great doors of the room, disclosing a saloon beyond; and they saw a table loaded with plate, and attended by servants in livery, while the chamberlain looked the image of triumph. Sir Howard was dismayed to cause so much trouble, and explained that he did not want dinner, but merely a little tea. The chamberlain bowed to the earth, then stepped forward, and lifted a massive silver cover from a dish on the table, exposing to the amazed Englishmen what seemed to be a pile of spinach swimming in butter, but which proved to be stewed tea. He apologised for the delay in serving it up, which had been caused by the difficulty of obtaining it, only one packet having been found in the whole city.

The two officers looked at the dish and at each other, and managed to keep from laughing, but politeness could not bring them to eat such a mess, and they knew not how to escape. A happy thought struck Sir Howard, and he hinted that they did not want the tea itself, but the water in which it had been boiled. Alas! the precious liquid had been thrown away; and nothing remained but to disappoint the chamberlain and go to bed tealess.

Next day the archbishop paid Sir Howard a visit of ceremony, as if he had been living in his own house; and he received visits from the nobility and magistrates of the neighbourhood, and the heads of the religious orders. The archbishop invited him to dinner, and he was met by a large company, including several *grandees*, who treated him with marked consideration. The banquet was served on plate, and presented everything that could tempt the palate, with Spanish fruit and flowers to lure the eye, while the saloon was thronged with servants and blazed with light. From the dinner the guests passed to a concert, embracing some excellent music, and the entertainment closed with a display of fireworks.

Next morning the chamberlain informed Sir Howard that he must now give a banquet to the archbishop, and invite the same company; but everything was to be done at the archbishop's expense. To this part of the proposal Sir Howard objected; but found that he could not pay the cost himself under the prelate's roof, and that his host would be wounded by any breach of the arrangements; so, he gave way, and the banquet was ordered, and the invitations sent out. All passed off as could be wished, eclipsing the success of the previous night, and the display of fireworks lit up the city.

The nobility vied with the archbishop in their attention to the commissioner, and the Count Mauda entertained him at a banquet followed by a concert, at which the band played a piece of music composed in his honour, while the company remained standing. Nor was he less appreciated by the religious orders. The friars of the San Martini monastery gave him a repast in their refectory, and a concert of sacred music, performed on two organs played together.

But the most singular attention he received was an invitation to a convent of Benedictine nuns, where he was served with a repast on plate, and admitted to a ball got up by the young ladies under education in the building. These *belles* invited him to join the dance as he looked on with admiring, and perhaps aspiring eyes, and overruled his plea that he was ignorant of the Spanish waltz by offering to become his teachers. He writes to Lady Douglas that he could not resist such an opportunity, and it is hardly necessary to add that a few lessons made him perfect.

The priesthood regarded him with such favour, that they threw open to him the palace of the Inquisition on his wishing to pay it a visit. Happily its functionaries had been suppressed, and he might think that the calamities of the French invasion were not too great a price for such a deliverance; for he passed the threshold reflecting how many had entered in terror, though dust now told that the pavement was seldom crossed. The empty chambers threw back his steps; the groined roofs echoed his voice: and he might think of the words of the prophet—

The stone shall cry out of the wall, and the beam out of the timber shall answer it.

Surely the second Philip would have looked for such a manifestation, if he thought of an heretic thus visiting the judgment hall, standing before the vacant tribunal, and having for his conductor a Spanish archbishop. Sir Howard gave a sigh to the victims of the institution as he looked on the gloomy pillars, and raised his eyes to the ceiling which had frowned back their appealing looks. He threaded the passages below, and explored the dungeons, reading the inscriptions on the walls, and he evinced such interest in these sad memorials, that the archbishop ordered them to be copied for him. They then visited the library, and he examined the forbidden books, amongst which he noted the French *Encyclopaedia*, the works of Voltaire and Frederick the Great, and a *History of the French Revolution*.

They proceeded from the Inquisition to the convent of Mosquiver, and were received by the whole sisterhood, who presented Sir Howard with a token of their handiwork, but what shape it took he does not mention. Nor did this visit conclude the day's engagements, as he spent the evening at the Countess of Poiega's, who held a grand *tertulia* in his honour.

The public institutions of Santiago included a college, divided between the army and civil service, one wing being assigned to civilians, and the other to cadets. Such an establishment naturally interested Sir Howard, who attached such importance to education; and he paid it an early visit. He found the military wing in decay, though it still supported masters, and offered the attraction of a good system. The cadets were few in number, but well trained, and went through their drill in a manner that elicited his praise. He determined to make an effort for the preservation of the establishment, and wrote to the Supreme *Junta* the same day, reminding it of the want of trained officers in their armies, and pointing to the college as their proper source, which would be cut off, if not liberally endowed.

Nor did he trust solely to his own representations, but obtained the co-operation of the archbishop and Mr. Ballusteros, the Secretary of the *Junta*, whom he invited to accompany him to the college, and they proceeded there the next morning. He paraded the cadets in their presence, and put them through their drill and such line movements as their small number permitted, both to show their proficiency and the advantage of such training. He afterwards marched them into the school-room, where they underwent an examination by the masters, followed by questions from himself; and this impressed the archbishop and Mr. Ballusteros with such an opinion of the institution, that they became its advocates with the government. Their intercession proved successful, and Sir Howard had the satisfaction of knowing that he had saved the college.

Such attention to the public interests extended his authority and spread his influence everywhere, for it was seen that he acted in the noblest spirit. But he understood the Spanish character, and knew the point beyond which it might be unsafe to step; so, he declined the command of the Alarms, which the Supreme *Junta* wished him to assume, and pointed out that a foreigner would be considered an intruder in such a position. But he undertook to organise the force, and laboured at this task incessantly, riding from one station to another, and assembling and reviewing the musters. Such acts showed his singleness of purpose and won him universal respect, adding to the weight of the English name, and making a watchword of his own.

Sir Howard did not leave Santiago without thanking the archbishop for his hospitality, and recognising the attention of his household, amongst whom he distributed a sum equal to what would have been his outlay at an inn. Their intercourse acquainted the archbishop with our national character in one of its best types, and this proved not unnecessary; for he was now to see it in another form. The strain came first on Sir Howard himself in the Spanish cantonments. Here he was visited by an English midshipman and boat's crew who had been wrecked on the coast, and fell into the hands of the French; but contrived to effect their escape, and arrived at the cantonments in company with an officer of hussars, much out at elbows.

The stranger had joined them on the way, and announced himself as Captain Charles Allen, of the 5th Hussars of the King's German Legion. He stated that he had been taken prisoner in action, and sent to the frontier, where he eluded the guard, and found shelter with a guerilla chief in Navarre; passing from him to a chief below, and so on till he met the midshipman. Such adventures as he had encountered!— and he told them in such a manner, so like what became Captain Allen, who was noted for his dash and vivacity. General Abadia invited him to dinner, and the Spanish officers were charmed by his bearing and stories, not knowing which to admire most. Sir Howard asked for his passport, and he produced it directly, calling attention to the signature of the guerilla chiefs, which confirmed his statements, though these spoke for themselves: and he gave Sir Howard such particulars about his own friends in the Legion, that he could have vouched for everything he said.

He might have enjoyed free quarters with the Spanish Army, but professed impatience to rejoin his corps; and Sir Howard advanced him forty pounds to cover his expenses. The hussar showed a proper sense of his kindness, but no more; and they parted the best of friends, and mutually pleased—Sir Howard with his new acquaintance, and the hussar with his forty pounds. But news came that he had made a raid on Santiago, and told the same story to the archbishop, from whom he extracted a sum equal to a hundred; and this raised a hue and cry. Sir Howard started a pursuit, but it was always behind the hussar, whom it just missed at Oporto, and again at Almeida, losing all trace of him at Lisbon. Of course, it was found that Captain Allen had not been absent from his regiment, and it remained uncertain whether his personator was a French spy or an English sharper.

Any mortification the incident caused must have been effaced from Sir Howard's mind on his arrival at Corunna, where he met the kindest reception, everyone seeking to do him honour. He was invited almost daily to entertainments, and received the most flattering tributes, which we may regret he has noted so briefly; for the details would have introduced us to Spanish society at an absorbing crisis. But what relates to himself is skimmed over, and we catch but a glimpse of his triumph in little *billets* to Lady Douglas. "I have been absolutely oppressed with honours and attentions," he writes. Yet it is plain that he enjoyed the outbreak, and Spanish gallantry knew how to make it acceptable. He writes again:

> At a most magnificent entertainment given me yesterday, a friend of mine, who has often heard me speak of you and our children, whispered the host; and your health was drunk in the English manner, and the toast was honoured with a discharge of fireworks and some excellent music. I will leave you to guess how I felt it.

Another letter tells her of a ball given by himself, and he takes credit for its success, though he appeals to have fully shared the pleasure of his guests.

> I gave a dance to the principal families, which I assure you went off very well. They danced till five o'clock, and I was obliged, of course, to see the last of it. The dances were waltzes and waltz-country-dances, which are very pretty, but which I hope never to see in England. Charles begins to waltz a little. I am no proficient, and kicked the ladies' feet.

Ladies will be shocked to hear that he had so soon forgotten his lessons at Santiago.

CHAPTER 16

Working the Guerillas

Sir Howard left the cantonments to visit the hospitals, now packed with sick, and obliged to turn numbers away. Only the kindest and bravest nature would have sought these sinks of misery, where suffering rotted in neglect—ear and eye were alike shocked—and the atmosphere reeked with infection. But he knew that his supervision was nowhere more required, and could be nowhere more beneficial; for he went to enforce cleanliness, and administer relief furnished by the English Government on his requisition. His judicious arrangements were most successful, and reduced the number of the sick in a surprising manner, while the supplies he distributed kept the remnant of the army in health. He writes to Lady Douglas:

> I will not shock your tender nature by any recital of the scenes I have witnessed. The timely arrival of supplies from England put it in my power to administer the only remedy; for nearly one-half the army was in the hospitals (if they can be called such), and the British Government may be assured that the succours I have distributed have saved at least 6,000 men.

This reference to his duties indicates their compass, but shows us nothing of their drudgery, which involved an amount of labour hardly credible. The pen was constantly in his hand, and he scarcely passed an hour without writing—now to Lord Wellington and Lord Liverpool; now to the Supreme *Junta*; and incessantly to General Abadia, the Guerilla chiefs, and the Captains of the Alarms. He maintained a correspondence with the Count of Amaranthe and General Bucella, commanding the Portuguese Armies,—with Generals Castaños and Mendizabal, and the Honourable Mr. Wellesley, the British Minister in Spain. His instructions required him to send Lord Wellington copies of all his letters and despatches, to whomsoever addressed, and to furnish duplicates to the Minister for War; while he had to keep a record of the disposal of every article of clothing in his charge, and every musket and cartridge issued to the Spanish levies.

He employed a number of spies, whose reports he forwarded to Lord Wellington, and thus supplied him with intelligence from every part of the country; but we see nothing of the labour this imposed but the result. It is true he had the assistance of a secretary, but much of the work was of a character that could only be executed by himself, and how little assistance he received is apparent when we find despatches copied in his letter-books in his own hand.

Nor was he one to think that he had done enough in discharging this routine; for he found time for further work, undertaking tasks that others would never have conceived. He made it one of his first duties to ascertain the amount of subsistence in the province, and the sources of the national revenue, as well as the manner in which it was expended. Such information could neither be sought without caution, nor obtained without difficulty; but he persevered in his inquiries, and succeeded in forming estimates that proved of the greatest service.

One of his devices against the French was a proclamation to their foreign soldiers, reminding them that England was fighting for the liberties of the world, and inviting them to come into the Spanish lines, and enrol themselves in her service, when they would receive a bounty according to their rank. This he printed in three languages— German, Italian, and French—and his spies dispersed it so effectually, that it brought over a number of Germans and Italians, who were despatched to England for employment in other regions.

His success recommended the measure to General Abadia, who began to form a similar corps for the Spanish service, and it numbered four hundred before Sir Howard heard of the proceeding. He instantly applied to the Supreme *Junta* to have it suppressed, representing that Spain could have no defenders like her own sons, and that the formation of such a body would produce the worst impression on the people. The *Junta* admitted his objection, and ordered the enrolment to be discontinued.

The measures he had taken to arm the population received the approval of the English Government, and Lord Liverpool engaged to furnish the Spanish authorities with arms and uniforms for 100,000 men, to be forwarded as fast as they could be obtained.

★★★★★★

Among other gratifying testimonies, Sir Howard received a letter from Colonel (afterwards Lord) Bloomfield, informing him of the approbation of the prince regent:—"You seem to have conducted the objects of your mission with great adroitness and success," writes Colonel Bloomfield, "and I have much satisfaction in assuring you that the prince speaks of you with great respect. No doubt your task is full of difficulties, but I know no one more likely to rise out of them than yourself."

★★★★★★

Vessels constantly arrived at Corunna with these supplies, and Sir Howard received them in store, and regulated their issue. He had suggested the fabrication of some small guns to be carried up mountains on the backs of mules, and used by the guerilla chiefs to dislodge the enemy from farm-buildings, where they were in the habit of taking refuge from their attacks; and these light pieces came out, and proved very serviceable in later operations.

He never lost sight of the work of organising the Alarms, and had now brought that force into good training, though he confined the drill to the simplest movements, and left the men to their own intelligence, after he had taught them to act in concert and support each other. He received a despatch from Lord Wellington in the midst of this work, begging to know whether General Abadia was in a position to move forward again, or whether he could undertake the defence of Galicia during the months of March and April, as this would relieve the English Army for other operations.

★★★★★★

Lord Wellington's despatch is dated Gallegos, Jan. 22nd, 1812, and is marked by Sir Howard as received on Feb. 2nd. The following is the passage relating to General Abadia:—Having taken Ciudad Rodrigo, it is very desirable that I should move from this quarter. If General Abadia cannot move forward, so as to divert the attention of the enemy from me, or from other quarters, can he in the months of March and April, when all the streams will be full, defend Galicia? Pray let me hear from you in answer to this question soon. The French are talking of moving in this direction, but they had not heard of the fall of Ciudad Rodrigo. If they move this way, I hope to give a good account of them.

Ever yours most sincerely,   Wellington.

★★★★★★

Sir Howard had no hope of animating General Abadia; but he proceeded to the Spanish quarters, and acquainted him with Lord Wellington's wishes. General Abadia made an evasive reply, and threw the
responsibility of deciding on Sir Howard. The commissioner wrote to
Lord Wellington:

I do not shrink from this, My Lord, but it would have been satisfactory to me, as well as to Your Lordship, to have had a more
explicit answer from him.

He then gives a view of the condition of the army, from which he
drew the conclusion that it could effect nothing; at the same time he
expressed the greatest reliance on the peasantry and the efforts of the
guerillas; he concludes:

And from these considerations, together with the impracticable
nature of the country at this season, and the scarcity of grain,
more than from dependence on the army, I should not feel
uneasy about Galicia during the months of March and April.
(Despatch to Lord Wellington, dated Feb. 4th, 1812.)

But he was not disposed to leave the issue to chance, and he set
to work to place it beyond doubt, aiming at such an organisation as
would prevent the French operating in Galicia, except with more
powerful means than they possessed, and also disable them from moving reinforcements against Lord Wellington. He concerted measures
of co-operation with the Count of Amaranthe, commanding the Portuguese Army, and combined these movements with those of Generals
Mendizabal, Porlier, and Poll, commanding in the Asturias, and with
the operations of the guerilla chiefs Minas, Longa, Palto, Campilza,
Sarazar, Sabzeda, and others, supporting all by the attitude of the
Alarms. He was everywhere seconded by the popular enthusiasm,
which rose to such a height that it could hardly be restrained, and the
people clamoured to be led against the enemy.

Such a movement of the irregular forces again aroused the jealousy
of General Abadia; and he complained of Sir Howard's supervision of
the Alarms, though undertaken at the request of the Supreme *Junta*,
declaring that it was a slight to the army.

★★★★★★

Mr. Ballusteros thus addressed him on the 1st of March:—"The
Supreme *Junta* has determined to request of you that, while visiting the Alarms of those provinces through which you intend

passing, you will condescend to propose the best method for regulating and superintending those bodies."

★★★★★★

Sir Howard would not allow such an impression to prevail, and ceased his personal interference, but continued to give counsel to the chiefs, and they carried out his orders with the greatest cheerfulness.

Lord Wellington was reassured by his promise for Galicia, and felt himself at liberty to undertake the siege of Badajos, on which he moved forthwith, sending him some general instructions, in connexion with the plan of operations he had conceived himself. This was at once put in train. General Mendizabal made a rapid movement towards the Douro, with the view of occupying the enemy in that part of the north of Spain, and the other regular corps assumed a menacing attitude at various points, while the enemy was everywhere harassed by the guerillas and Alarms.

His columns were pounced upon when they most reckoned on security, in the middle of the night and the broad day, in the mountain pass and the open plain, the Spaniards being invisible till a discharge of carbines announced their presence, or till they galloped through the French ranks. Many of these achievements were of an heroic character, and retrieved for the nation the renown lost by its generals. Longa, Minas, and Cruchaja united the Navarrese division of Alarms in an attack on General Abbe, which ended in his flying, from the field, leaving behind two pieces of cannon and 600 dead. Longa writes to Sir Howard:

They were pursued for two leagues, and only owed their safety to the darkness. (Despatch of Don Francisco Longa to Sir Howard Douglas, in the *Douglas Papers*.)

Maceda headed the guerillas at Porto San Payo, and joined an English frigate in an attack on the corps of Marshal Ney, which they drove from its position, after inflicting a severe loss. Salazar led his band against the town of Sasamon, which he captured, and put the enemy to the sword. (Despatch of Don Francisco Salazar to Sir Howard Douglas, in the *Douglas Papers*.) Duran took three towns by assault without an open breach. The town of Tudela was garrisoned by 1,000 men, supported by a division of 3,000 foot and 600 horse under the orders of Generals Avi and Panatier.

It was defended by two forts, and contained a train of artillery, brought from Saragossa, comprising fifteen heavy guns, 16-, 18-, and

24-pounders, a 9-inch mortar, six 7-inch howitzers, and two royal howitzers. By adroit movements and counter-marches Duran succeeded in deceiving Generals Avi and Panatier, as well.as the garrisons of Logrono and Lodon, and cut off the communications of the town. At nine in the evening Colonel Tahiena led the battalion of Rioji and the light regiment of Soria under the walls of the garden of the barefooted Carmelites, and there planted the scaling ladders, which he was the first to mount.

He reached the garden unobserved, and formed the troops into companies, when they seem to have been discovered; for the enemy sounded the attack as he dashed into the town. The Place de los Toros was defended by artillery, but such was the impetuosity of the Spaniards that a quarter of an hour sufficed to capture the guns, and put the French to the rout. Lieutenant Tabaenca rushed at the Gate of Vitella at the same moment, with forty men, and made prisoners of the guard, throwing open the gate and thus admitting the remainder of the Spanish force. The French were obliged to take refuge in the fortified barrack of Santa Clara, and the Spaniards retired from the town, after they had burnt the military stores and spiked the guns, though they carried off the mortars and howitzers. (Despatch of Don Josef Duran to Sir Howard Douglas, in the *Douglas Papers*.)

A dashing movement by Minas on the Aragon was witnessed by Sir Howard, who had the satisfaction of seeing the French turn their backs, with a heavy loss in killed and wounded. Minas followed at the double, obliging them to seek the shelter of the town of Losada, where they held fortified houses, while the Spaniards ravaged the country up to Pampeluna. Minas then crossed the mountains in search of Soulier, though worn out with fatigue and almost famishing. The march was conducted with such secrecy that the French general was in bed when a heavy fire of musketry announced his presence. Soulier's force consisted of 1,600 infantry and 170 cavalry, posted in the town of Sangrassa; the Spanish chief writes to Sir Howard:

And he formed his infantry with his usual coolness and valour, notwithstanding the surprise, and the loss he had sustained.

The Spaniards had seized the bridge, and his first object was to drive them from this point, which he attempted directly, leading the attack himself. Minas allowed him to advance within pistol-shot, and then opened on him with his field-gun and a volley of musketry, by which his column was almost destroyed. But he retained his coolness, threw himself into the broken ranks, and maintained a running fight for five hours, effecting a retreat to Sos, and wresting the highest praise from his brave enemy. (Despatch of General Minas to Sir Howard Douglas, in the *Douglas Papers*.) The loss of the French was 900 killed and wounded, Soulier himself being hit; while that of the Spaniards was only 200 wounded and 30 killed, including four officers.

Minas again left his fastness in the mountains at the beginning of April, and accomplished a march of fifteen leagues in one day, with the intention of intercepting a French convoy, escorted by 150 cavalry and 2,000 infantry composed of Poles and the Imperial Guard. He showed himself near Victoria, and caused letters to be dispersed in the town intimating that he was on his way to the Pyrenees, but he had no thought of such a movement, and made a forced march to Artaban, where he took post unobserved.

His force was so placed as to form a circle, which would surround the convoy on its coming up, as well as the escort, but he gave an order that no man should molest the convoy till the escort was defeated. The French were seen approaching in a careless way, without suspecting an ambush, the high rocks concealing the Spaniards, who did not present themselves till a shower of balls had thrown the escort in confusion. They tried to rally, but the Spaniards now poured over the rocks and charged them with the bayonet, completing their rout. Minas writes to Sir Howard:

> The haughty Poles and Imperial Guard, being completely dismayed, threw away their arms and fell victims on our bayonets.

The carnage in this action was dreadful, and Minas informed Sir Howard that not one of the French would have escaped only for the vicinity of the castle of Artaban. To this fortress about 800 made good their retreat, after a loss of nearly 600 killed, 500 wounded, and 150 prisoners. Among the killed was Deslandes, Cabinet Secretary to King Joseph; and the captives included his wife, Donna Carlotta Ariana, who was wounded, and two other ladies, with five children. The spoil embraced 100 waggons, two standards, the military chest of the Polish regiment of infantry, the correspondence of King Joseph, which Deslandes was conveying to France, the carriage and valuables of Deslandes, and eight drums. (Despatch of General Minas to Sir Howard Douglas, in the *Douglas Papers*.)

Such were some of the achievements of the irregular forces during the time that Sir Howard undertook to hold Galicia, and occupy the

French in the north of Spain. They had the effect desired, in keeping lord Wellington from being embarrassed at a critical period; and Sir Howard received a despatch from Lord Fitzroy Somerset towards the end of April, announcing the capture of Badajoz.

The guerilla successes exasperated the French, who resorted to the severest reprisals, and the peasants returned from their forays to find their homes devastated and their wives and daughters dishonoured and sometimes butchered. These atrocities were so common that they are mentioned as things of course by the guerilla chiefs in their despatches to Sir Howard. But he relates one enormity that drove them to madness, and excites a shudder even at this distance of time.

The French desired to occupy a monastery commanding a strong pass, but admission was denied by the monks, who made a stout resistance. They were overcome; and the French punished their temerity by roasting several of them, and putting the rest to the sword. A party of the French afterwards fell into the hands of the guerillas, who obtained possession of an immense oven constructed for the use of a regiment, and baked them alive. Such are the horrors of invasion!

CHAPTER 17

Serving with the Spanish Army

The enthusiasm of the Alarms and guerillas at these successes was damped by the absence of Sir Howard, who no longer superintended their musters and drills. He continued to furnish them with arms, and to correspond with their chiefs, directing the movement with the same zeal, but he was not seen at their posts. They had become so used to his presence that the change excited remark; and a rumour spread that the government had forbidden him to attend. The sensation produced showed the popularity he had attained, and how completely he had won their confidence. Addresses poured in upon him from all parts, (a translation of one of these addresses is given in the Appendix); exasperated crowds paraded the streets of the towns; and the Alarms broke up from their masters with threatening cries.

The military became frightened at these demonstrations, and proposed that the bands should be disarmed; effecting this measure in several villages, though at such risk that it was carried no further. Indeed, the Supreme *Junta* ordered it to be discontinued, and the arms to be restored, at the same time censuring the generals; and they begged Sir Howard to resume his inspections of the Alarms, of the interruption of which they now first heard.

But he felt that such a course would confirm the popular impression, and widen the breach with the army, which he desired to heal; and he convinced the *Junta* that it would be better to give out that he was kept away from the musters by his other duties, which might be said with truth.

He was always ready to renounce himself, and never more so than now; for it was important to avoid offending General Abadia, whom he wished to join in some operations on the Esla. He had put the army in a serviceable condition, supplying it with arms and clothing; and the influence he thus acquired had been exerted to push forward its training. His withdrawal from the supervision of the Alarms gratified General Abadia, and the reason he pleaded for the step screened him from blame, and soothed the people; so that he preserved his influence with both, while he calmed the jealousies a foreigner naturally provoked.

This appeared on his next visit to the camp, when General Abadia received him with compliments; and he might feel proud that one so prejudiced acknowledged his services, and expressed appreciation of what he had done for Spain. He paid the general a tribute in return, crediting him with the improved efficiency of the army, and then unfolded the plan of Lord Wellington, which contemplated the advance of the division of General Castaños, to co-operate with the Galician Army on the Orbigo and Esla, and keep the French in that quarter employed. He entreated Abadia to act at once, and the general replied that he had but one objection, his want of artillery, which Sir Howard could not deny justified inaction.

He determined to see if some equipment could not be obtained, and hastened back to Corunna; but his hopes fell as he entered the arsenal, and beheld the lately-deserted foundries ringing with the sound of the anvil, and sending up volumes of smoke; for his knowledge of the ruling powers made him look for disappointment in what others might have thought encouraging. He dreaded another expedition to America; and inquiry confirmed his fears, eliciting that this was the destination of a battery of artillery there, comprising just the pieces wanted by the Galician Army. It stood ready for shipment, and an order came to prepare a number of gun-carriages for the same service while he was questioning the artificers.

He considered whether it might be possible to avert the shipment, and secure the artillery for General Abadia; but his functions did not extend to political transactions, and he could only approach the Regency by a report to Sir Henry Wellesley, who resided at Cadiz, and would receive it too late for use. It suddenly occurred to him to make an application for the guns without appearing to know their destination. He instantly acquainted the *Junta* and General Castaños with the wants of the Galician Army, and represented that here was the very equipment required, begging that it might be issued for service. (Despatch of Sir Howard Douglas to the Earl of Liverpool.)

General Castaños had now entered Galicia, and announced that he was crippled by the same deficiency, which he entreated him to correct by securing the battery in question.

★★★★★★

Since artillery of the competent calibre in proportion to the object is indispensable, I have great satisfaction in learning that through your means I can reckon upon a train which till now I had been in want of, and not to lose time I have advised the commandant of the artillery of the army to repair to Corunna, to dispose its immediate departure for Lugo, trusting that you, who know the necessity of this arm, will contribute to lessen the difficulties that may retard its leaving that place,—Despatch of General Castaños to Sir Howard Douglas, in the *Douglas Papers.*

★★★★★★

Sir Howard rode off with his letter to Mr. Ballusteros, the Secretary of the Supreme *Junta*, and learnt that the *Junta* had made inquiries about the guns, and were incensed to find that they were to be despatched to the colonies, although paid for out of the Galician revenue. The battery was embarked the same day for Ferrol, where a Spanish frigate waited to convoy it to America; and the regency added to its folly by again diverting the best troops of General Abadia to the same service. These regiments had been armed with muskets and carbines furnished by England, and were partly clothed from the English supplies. (Despatch of Sir Howard Douglas to Sir Henry Wellesley.)

The people could hardly be kept from insurrection when this proceeding became known; and it created a division in the government itself, for the Bishop of Reufe seceded from the regency to mark his disapproval of the step; and the Supreme *Junta* made a protest against the continuance of the American struggle while the French remained on Spanish soil. Sir Howard failed to stop the enterprise, but had aroused opposition, and the part he took increased his popularity and influence. On the other hand, every day gave proof of the madness of the government, for their armies were perishing of hunger at the moment that they despatched this expedition; and its cost left them without means to pay for a cargo of flour which arrived at Corunna for their use. ("Their daily existence may be considered a miracle."—Despatch of General Castaños to Sir Howard Douglas.)

The arrival of General Castaños in Galicia inspired hopes that he would render material support to Lord Wellington in the campaign about to open, and Sir Howard hastened to secure his co-operation as soon as he could leave Corunna. The object he thought of greatest consequence was the reduction of Astorga, which would deprive the

French of a most important post; and he urged this with such force that General Castaños assembled a council of war to consider the project. Reference was made to the commanding officer of the artillery, and he reported that the army possessed no means of undertaking such an operation, which the council found to be perfectly true, and declared that it could not be entertained.

Sir Howard knew the inadequacy of the artillery, but felt persuaded that means of attack did exist, though in a small way, and he considered how he should proceed to get them applied to the purpose. Could he expect that the statement of his views would have any result but to excite professional resentment, when it set his opinion against the verdict of a council of war? He saw the difficulty of moving, but he also saw the great importance, and he determined to open the subject privately to his friend General Giron, the Chief of the Staff. The general met it in the best spirit, with a sincere desire to promote the credit of the army, and see it efficiently employed.

Sir Howard quickly convinced him of the advantages to he gained; and he acknowledged that the town would add to the security of Galicia, and must even oblige the French to evacuate the Asturias. But Astorga had made a long stand against Junot at the head of a French Army, which gave it a repute for capabilities of defence, and he pronounced the want of artillery a fatal bar. Sir Howard stated that this might be remedied, and adverted to his recent visit to the arsenal, where he had seen six brass 16-pounders, with carriages, which were available for service, though not in the best condition; and he engaged to supply a brigade of five-and-a-half howitzers from the English stores as a further equipment.

The arsenal contained abundant materials for the construction of waggons and trucks, and he entreated the general to go to Corunna, and form his own judgment of what could be obtained, giving him directions where to look for everything he had mentioned, and even drawings of the places where they were stowed.

General Giron secretly left the cantonments the same evening, went to Corunna by post, and returned, satisfied. Sir Howard now told him that he had served in the artillery, and his experience enabled him to say that the means available for the siege were adequate, which he begged him to impress on General Castaños, and get the question reconsidered. The general acted on his advice, and gained over General Castaños, who carried the point with the council of war. Orders were given for the necessary preparations, and they were pushed on with vigour, though some delay arose from want of money—as important a sinew as artillery. But energy overcame all difficulties, and 16,000 men marched on Astorga.

Sir Howard announced the expedition to the Count of Amaranthe, as well as to General Bucella, and warned them to guard the country left open; but Lord Wellington made a movement that relieved them of this duty, just as their advance obliged the French to retire.

★★★★★★

Lord Wellington informed Sir Howard of this arrangement in the following despatch:—

Guinaldo, May 25, 1812.

I received yesterday your letter of the 18th instant, and I had at the same time one of the 20th from the Conde d'Amaranthe, from which I learnt that the enemy, after plundering the villages on the frontier of Galicia, had retired to Benevente.

There is no chance of their attacking Galicia as long as this army shall be on this frontier; and entertaining this opinion and feeling an anxious desire that the Portuguese Government should be saved the expense of the militia in arms, when not necessary to be incurred) and that the individuals composing the militia should have the advantage of returning to their homes when their services shall not be required, I desired that the militia should be disbanded as soon as I brought back the army to this quarter, with the exception of those corps necessary to observe the enemy's movements. They are, however, ready to turn out again at a moment's notice.

I have the honour to be, &c.,

Wellington.

Lieut.-Col. Sir Howard Douglas, Bart.

★★★★★★

The same intelligence set in motion the guerilla parties and Alarms; and Merino took advantage of the diversion to sweep across the track of a French column engaged in levying a contribution of meat in the district of Penaranda. He planted his infantry on some heights cutting the line of march, and surrounded the French as they came up, first riddling their ranks with a volley of musketry. His cavalry seized the only gap for retreat, leaving them no resource but to surrender, and they laid down their arms amidst a heap of dead and wounded. Merino sallied the victory by a massacre, which the atrocities perpetrated by the French provoked, but do not excuse. He singled out 110 of his captives to be shot on the field, and carried out their execution in the most solemn manner, prefacing it with this speech:—

I inflict this chastisement for the horrible sacrifice of the three members of the Royal Supreme *Junta* of the province of Burgos, whom the French surprised on the 20th at Grando, and put to an infamous death at Soria and Aranda, hanging them afterwards to a gallows, where they still remain, for no other crime than that of having taken an active part in defence of their country, so unjustly invaded, pillaged, and insulted by these monsters. (Despatch of Don Geronimo Merino to Sir Howard Douglas.)

The French sent out a column to intercept the victors and rescue the prisoners, but their design came to Merino's knowledge, and a lonely cross-road enabled him to plant an ambuscade. The usual volley of musketry too late revealed the danger, and they fled in confusion, throwing away their arms, and leaving an addition of 200 to Merino's captives, instead of recovering those in his possession. (Despatches of Sir Howard Douglas to the Earl of Wellington and Sir Henry Wellesley.)

This was the moment chosen by the Spanish Regency to order another detachment of troops to be embarked for South America. It transpired that a larger body would have been sent before, only for the obstacles raised by Sir Howard, and he endeavoured to induce General Castaños to suspend the embarkation of the present force until the measure could be reconsidered. The general convinced him that he could not delay, as his orders were imperative, and the troops were sent off to Vigo the same day. But Sir Howard prevented their embarkation, (see note following), and his interference obtained the approbation of the English Minister in Spain: Sir Henry Wellesley wrote:

Your endeavours to defeat a measure so injurious to the interests of Galicia, cannot fail to be approved by the Government of His Royal Highness the Prince Regent, and you will do right to use every exertion to defeat any project of the kind in future. (Despatch of the Hon. Sir Henry Wellesley, K.B., to Sir Howard Douglas. See note below.)

★★★★★★

Nevertheless, so strange a people are the Spaniards, that a second expedition against the colonies, having with it all the field artillery just supplied by England, would have sailed from Vigo but for the prompt interference of Sir Howard Douglas.—*Pen-*

insular War, vol, v.

Lord Liverpool was equally satisfied with his proceedings. His secretary writes to Sir Howard from the War Department on the 15th of May:—"His Lordship has learned with great regret that the Spanish authorities have persisted in the very impolitic measure of sending troops from Galicia to their American colonies, and he desires me to convey to you his full approbation of the conduct you have held upon this delicate occasion."

★★★★★★

But the party of the regency did not regard his proceedings with the same favour, and an incident happened at the time which enabled its adherents to show their bad feeling. A convoy of reinforcements for Lord Wellington was met by a storm on its way to Lisbon, damaging one of its transports, which took refuge in Corunna Bay; and Sir Howard's thoughtful kindness prompted him to apply to the Governor of Corunna for permission to bring the soldiers ashore. He made the request as a matter of form, not dreaming of objection; but faction easily raises difficulties, and General Taboada replied that it would be a breach of his orders to permit the landing of foreign troops.

Sir Howard reminded him that these troops must be regarded as allies and defenders, and begged him to refer the question to General Abadia, whose sentiments the governor knew to be his own, and accepted him as arbiter. The general decided that the soldiers might be put ashore in the daytime, on the other side of the bay, but that they must land without their arras. Such a proposal seemed an insult, and Sir Howard received it in a manner becoming a British officer—declining the favour, and assuring the governor that the terms prescribed should never be divulged to the soldiers who had come to the succour of Spain.

The same feelings met Sir Howard at other points. Lord Wellington's plan for the campaign embraced operations to the north by the Spanish forces, based on a depot of stores to be established on the coast; and he directed him to report on the fitness of the Bayonne Islands for this service. He went to fulfil this duty, notifying his object to the governor of the district, and apprising him of Lord Wellington's orders. But the projects of the English general carried no weight with that officer, and he declined to permit the survey, alleging that it might be used to the disadvantage of Spain in the event of a war with England. Such an objection seemed monstrous at a moment when the two nations were so closely allied, and could only have been started by faction.

Happily, it was disavowed by General Castaños, who removed all obstructions, and Sir Howard made an inspection of the whole coast. His examination led him to the conclusion that the spot marked by Lord Wellington was not suited for a base of operations, and he suggested that the depot should be established at the island of Arosa, which afforded the requisite facilities. Lord Wellington wrote in reply:

> I concur with you in your opinion of the advantages of the island of Arosa over the Bayonne Islands. (Despatch of the Earl of Wellington to Sir Howard Douglas, April 20, 1812.)

But it became necessary to refer the point to Lord Liverpool, as the occupation of the island involved an outlay of 10,000*l.* for the construction of works of defence. Sir Howard had before recommended Lord Liverpool to send out a squadron to operate in this quarter in conjunction with English marines, which would enable him to furnish supplies to the guerillas in Navarre and Biscay by a direct channel, at the same time that it cut off the water communications of the French, and opened a way for turning their positions if they resorted to a line of defence between the Ebro.

He now received intelligence that Lord Liverpool had adopted his views, having fitted out a squadron with great secrecy and despatched it to the Spanish waters, with a battalion of marines and a company of artillery, and Commodore Sir Home Popham arrived at Corunna to consult him on its movements. The commodore's letter reached him at the cantonments, and he instantly sought General Castaños, as little could be effected without his concurrence, while it was desirable that he should understand the objects in view.

The general promised to join him and the commodore on the following day, and Sir Howard took post for Corunna to prepare—visiting Sir Home as soon as he arrived. He found him on board his own old ship, the *Venerable*, and learnt that he had left the rest of the squadron at sea, to prevent any warning reaching the French.

He had discovered Sir Howard's value in the Walcheren expedition, and now declared that he could not act with effect unless he accompanied the squadron, as nothing but his authority would draw around it the guerillas and peasantry. Such a service held out great attractions to Sir Howard, and he also wished to give the commodore his support, but did not feel at liberty to move without the orders of Lord Wellington. They referred the point to General Castaños on his arrival, and he recommended him to go, adverting to the effect his appearance would produce on the guerillas, and promising to keep the French employed in his absence. His arguments removed Sir Howard's objections, for they had already occurred to himself, and he had only hesitated from a fear that his judgment might be swayed by his wishes. But he did not shrink from the responsibility now that he felt satisfied as to his duty, and it was settled that he should accompany Sir Home.

★★★★★★

Sir Howard's conception of this expedition is thus mentioned by Napier:—"Sir Howard Douglas, observing the success of the enemy in cutting off the Partidos from the coast, and the advantage they derived from the water communication—considering also that, if Lord Wellington should make any progress in the coming campaign, new lines of communication with the sea would be desirable—proposed that a powerful squadron, with a battalion of marines and a battery of artillery, should be secretly prepared for a littoral warfare on the Biscay coast. This suggestion was approved of, and Sir Home Popham was sent from England in May."—*Peninsular War*, vol. v.

★★★★★★

Arrangements were made to prevent inconvenience from his absence. He gave over the stores to Commissary-General White, directing him to continue their issue, and obey the requisitions of General Castaños, and he empowered the general to apply for whatever he needed. Proper communications were addressed to other authorities, and to the principal guerilla chiefs; and Sir Howard received a note from General Castaños enjoining all the functionaries of the government to afford him every assistance. He embarked with great privacy, and a fair wind carried the *Venerable* out of the harbour on her errand of succour and deliverance.

CHAPTER 18

Takes the Field

The French obtained information of the arrival of a British squadron, in spite of the endeavours to keep it secret, and the appearance of the *Venerable* on the coast was the signal for their abandoning several posts. Sir Howard proposed to take advantage of the westerly wind to reach Beruca de Lecitia, and open communication with Don Gaspar, a guerilla chief, as his support might enable them to attack a strong post at Le Cintio Rey. (Sir Howard's despatches do not mention the chief's surname, but always speak of him as Don Gaspar.) On the 17th of June they came up with the other vessels of the squadron, in a stiff breeze, off Cape Mechichaco, and all pushed out to sea to avoid the swell near the shore.

Two days passed before this subsided, when they stood in under the Cape, and boats were sent into the bay in the evening to cut out all craft that could be useful in landing troops. The operation was effected with great gallantry, under a fire from the French, though they evacuated the place when the boats regained the ships, retiring in the direction of Le Cintio Rey. The squadron shaped its course for the same place, while the seizure of the shore boats spread the fact of its presence over the country without the aid of messengers.

Such a result had been anticipated on board, and Sir Howard and the commodore felt no surprise next morning to see a boat put off from under an abutting cliff and come alongside, bringing a guerilla officer. He announced himself as Don Gaspar's second in command, and reported that the chief had conjectured that the squadron would attack Le Cintio, and was ready to give his co-operation, but thought it well to point out that they were close to the French frontier, and that the commodore must be prepared to afford him and his men a refuge on board the ships, if the enemy came upon them from the rear.

119

Sir Howard reassured him on this point, and arranged that Don Gaspar should appear before the place on the following day, when the squadron would be present to share the attack. He recommended that a party should be stationed near the beach with draught oxen, in case of its being found desirable to land guns; and the officer promised compliance, hastening off to prepare his chief.

The day opened unpromisingly; for the vicinity of the squadron alarmed the French, and they sent off for reinforcements, while Don Gaspar had to march from a distance, and the roads were almost impassable. Hours elapsed without any sign of his appearance, and the weather was growing bad, making it dangerous for the ships to approach the shore, when the guerillas were seen crowning the heights about four in the afternoon. Sir Howard feared the effect of any failure to back them at the outset, particularly after placing them in so perilous a situation; for the French might be expected to hasten up a flying column from the rear to cut them off, and hence he would have fulfilled the compact at almost any risk. Fortunately, the commodore shared his sentiments, and stood in for the shore as soon as a lull of the breeze lessened the swell.

The works consisted of a fortified convent and a redoubt, and the guerillas effected the investment on the land side, while the *Venerable* was brought into position for bombarding the convent, and Sir Howard took post on her lower deck to watch the play of her guns. Some of the other ships came up, and they opened a cannonade; but the convent stood on a hill, and it was impossible to afford the guns the necessary elevation.

Sir Howard felt more scandalised at the bad gunnery, which made him tremble for the laurels of the navy; and he now conceived his scheme for introducing improvements and leavening the service with trained gunners. He looked over the guns to see how the lines were laid, and what approach was made to accuracy in allowing for the rolling of the ship, and then ascertained the different points in the disturbing effects of the motion, gathering the conclusions which formed the basis of his famous treatise.

So quick were his conceptions, that the idea of writing it flashed upon him at the same time, but did not divert him from the claims of the moment, and he went on deck to recommend a change in the mode of attack. This had been suggesting itself to Sir Home Popham, and they decided that a force from the *Surveillante* should take possession of an island facing the town with a carronade and mortar, and that a hundred seamen from the *Venerable* should land on the beach with a 24-pounder, for the purpose of breaching the redoubt. The gun might be dragged up a hill opposite the work, as the guerillas were at hand with the oxen, and Sir Howard's forethought in suggesting this provision now struck all. The hill was of about the same elevation as the one occupied by the redoubt, and the 24-pounder could open here, while the pieces on the island engaged the convent.

The guerillas received orders to protect the spot with a breastwork, which they promptly threw up, though opposed by a fire from the redoubt and convent, as well as from advanced parties of the enemy, posted in enclosures and the skirts of the town. A hawser was attached to the trunnions of the gun on reaching the beach, and the seamen drew it through the surf and looped it to the horns of the oxen, when the guerillas lent their aid, the sailors again gave their strong arms, and the united force ran it up the hill.

Here the seamen placed it in position, in spite of the enemy's fire, and made good practice on firm ground, silencing the French 18-pounders, and effecting a breach before sunset. The guerillas rushed to the assault, but the French met them with the same valour, and they reeled a little, borne back by the clash. But they quickly rallied, and dashed on with cheers, disappearing in the dense smoke, which rose in clouds, and enveloped the breach. An instant more decided the struggle, and the air rang with cries as they put the defenders to the sword.

The 24-pounder turned its fire on the convent from this time, and was supported by the guns on the island, while the enemy's advanced parties were driven in by a party of English marines firing from an eminence there, and by the guerillas. The French held out till next day, but then surrendered at discretion. Just as a party told off for storming; Sir Howard recommended the convent to be destroyed, to prevent its re-occupation, and the seamen carried out the operation under his orders, placing barrels of gunpowder under the strongest parts and blowing them into the air.

The explosion announced the event to a French column of eleven hundred men, hurrying up from Bilboa as a reinforcement, and which had arrived within two leagues. From a neighbouring height they saw the squadron sail away with the captured garrison, while the guerillas vanished, leaving them uncertain where they would appear next.

The ships came to anchor off Bermi at six o'clock in the evening of the 23rd, and Sir Howard and the commodore landed with a party of marines, and prepared to attack the fortified convent and batteries.

But the French evacuated the works without firing a shot, leaving behind their ammunition and numerous pieces of artillery, with a large quantity of provisions. The food was distributed among the poor, the guns disabled, and the convent blown up.

A force from the *Sparrow* and *Rhine* landed at the same time, and captured the neighbouring post of Plencia, where they also spiked the guns and destroyed the battery and guard-houses.

Two intercepted letters informed Sir Howard that the operations of the squadron caused the greatest alarm to the enemy up to the frontier of France, while they gave corresponding encouragement to the guerillas and Generals Benevales, Mendizabal, and Porlier, commanding the Spanish troops. Communications were established with the generals, and Sir Howard issued a circular, (see note following), to the guerilla chiefs, urging them to increased action and vigilance. This was dispersed over the country, from the Pyrenees to the gates of Madrid, and united all the guerilla bands in the efforts about to be made. (In a return in the *Douglas Papers* the guerilla force thus put in motion is estimated at 28,000 infantry and 8,000 cavalry. It fell off after Sir Howard's departure for England, and was very weak in the next campaign, when the allied army had gained possession of a great part of the country.)

★★★★★★

The circular is given here to show the manner in which Sir Howard brought the irregular troops to act in concert:—

On board H.B.M.S. *Venerable*, North Coast of Spain, 25th June, 1812.

Sir,

Circumstances very important to the common cause, and which cannot be trusted to a letter, oblige me to call your attention to the following operations. I am not only invested with the authority of your government to execute them, but I am also the Commissioner of Great Britain, by whoso hands quantities of arms and ammunition have been liberally distributed to assist you in combating the common enemy. I therefore have no doubt that you will consent to obey these recommendations.

First, it is of the highest importance that a strict watch be kept over Burgos, Victoria, and Torre la Vega, and speedy advices of whatever movements the enemy's forces may make in those quarters despatched to General Mendizabal and to Brigadiers Porlier and Longa.

Secondly. The small garrisons are to be equally watched and threatened in a way to oblige them to remain within their quarters, which, if they attempt to abandon, must be immediately destroyed.

In case the enemy should make any movement towards the coast, the *partidas* must follow them closely, harass their rear-guards, cut off their provisions, intercept their correspondence and communications, and in all manner possible work their ruin.

I have no doubt that your well-known patriotism, bravery, and activity will now be exercised in a surpassing manner, and I venture to promise you with the greatest confidence the most happy results.

Inconsequence I have resolved that you should, with the troops under your command, keep yourself in readiness from the 7th July till the 20th of the same month, or till new advice.

I have the honour to be, Sir,

Your most obedient humble servant,

Howard Douglas.

★★★★★★

The squadron stood into Porto Bay, and a party landed from the *Lyra* to destroy the batteries at the entrance of Bilboa Bar, under the guns of the *Rover* and *Sparrow*, supported by the frigate *Medusa*. The *Venerable* bore up with the *Surveillante* and *Rhine* at seven in the evening, and put ashore the marines of the three ships, with Sir Howard, the commodore, and Brigadier-General Carrol. The enemy did not wait for their attack, but hastily abandoned the batteries, which the sailors and marines destroyed, as well as the castles of Gulea and Begma, and rendered the guns useless by knocking off their trunnions. Another party laid barrels of powder under the barracks and guard-houses, and blew them into the air. This dashing enterprise was accomplished in an hour and a half, and the marines and sailors regained the ships without the smallest casualty.

Spies reported that a strong force had moved on Argolta, and next morning brought off the *alcalde* with a message from the French general. The poor magistrate was in great terror, and the message excused his trepidation, for it informed the commodore and the English commissioner that he was to be hanged and the town burnt if the squadron molested the French. Sir Howard told him that nothing would be done to compromise the town, unless the French broke its neutrality by firing the first shot, when they must acknowledge that they draw the attack on themselves, and hold him blameless.

The French had arrived in the last stage, of fatigue, and sank down exhausted in the batteries, but sprang to their guns on the approach of the *Lyra* brig, and opened a cannonade. They had now violated the understanding, and the ships replied by a bombardment which obliged them to fly from the town, and left them no time to execute their threats. Yet the *alcalde* may have partly owed his escape to his own prudence; for he took care to keep out of the way of the general, who went off mad with rage, and not indisposed to hang a few Spaniards.

It is a proof of the organisation established at this time through Spain that Sir Howard's circular reached Longa, many leagues in the interior, and brought an answer by his second in command within a few days. This officer was Colonel Alvarez, himself a noted leader, and he described their force as consisting of four thousand infantry and two hundred cavalry, which he engaged to present on the heights behind Castro Diobiale on the afternoon of the 6th of July. The squadron was to make its appearance at the same time, and lend its aid in an attack on the place, reputed of great strength and suitably garrisoned.

Bad weather kept the ships from the coast for the next few days, but the *Lyra* contrived to land some arms and artillery which Sir Howard had engaged to send General Benivales, and to arrange that he and the other Spanish generals should meet him at Camillas on the 2nd. The commodore stood in close to Lantino, that Sir Howard might reconnoitre the position, and they were unmolested from the shore, though a sloop ran under the batteries on their approach, and hoisted her colours, at the same time firing a gun. He had drawn a plan of the works from information, and now finished it correctly, ascertaining that the batteries were of a very formidable character, particularly to the westward of a promontory commanding the sandy beach, where attacking troops must land.

They sheered off on the completion of the reconnaissance, and he went to hold a conference with the Spanish generals at Camillas, according to his arrangement, by the. *Lyra*. It had leaked out that he was to come, and a crowd waited on the beach, and saluted him with acclamations. They formed his escort to the house of the principal resident, who met him at the door, and received him with the greatest cordiality. He became his guide round the town, and took him to a spot from which he could reconnoitre the neighbourhood, still under the command of the French, though not occupied. Evening drew on without bringing the generals, and he proposed to stay with his host for the night, not doubting that they would arrive next day.

His words reached the ear of a French spy loitering in the adjoining room, and he stole out of the house, mounted a horse, and carried the news to the French. The opportunity of capturing such a prisoner threw the commanding officer into ecstasies, and he concerted his measures at once, waiting impatiently for night. Then he silently mustered his corps and made a swoop on the town. They found all still; not a soul appeared in the streets, and they came unobserved to the house under the guidance of the spy. But their caution proved of no avail; for the host had represented the danger to Sir Howard, who had abandoned his intention, and was now comfortably asleep in the *Venerable*.

It appeared that the generals had been prevented attending by the vigilance of the French, and a messenger informed them that Sir Howard would proceed to St. Vincente de la Barquera, where they could meet without risk. But he was to have another narrow miss before he reached St. Vincente, and the incident may be mentioned as an instance of his presence of mind, while it shows how he retained his youthful activity. Two seamen had been posted in a boat attached to the stern for steerage, and the *Venerable* was wearing ship in a squall, when the rope broke, and it became very difficult to pick up the boat and men.

A creaking noise attracted Sir Howard as he watched the proceedings, and he turned to see a large brass gun break loose, and tilt in a manner that seemed to leave him no escape from destruction. There was not time for a second thought, and he instantly made a spring and leaped over the gun, which dashed to the lee quarter, and would have jammed him into a mummy there but for his prompt movement.

The governor and his staff came down to meet him at St. Vincente, and they were joined by Generals Mendizabal and Porlier, with the chief of his staff and he had now the satisfaction of learning that they had received all his communications and agreed in his suggestions, so that every precaution had been taken to insure the objects of the expedition. Such was the footing on which he had established himself with the Spanish officers, who originally regarded him with jealousy, and mistrusted his counsels. The success of his measures had won their confidence, and gave weight to whatever he proposed, while his kind and unassuming manner disarmed ill-will, and made everybody his friend.

He recommended General Mendizabal to leave General Porlier in observation of Torre la Viga, and muster all his force against Andrea, passing on to attack Viga as soon as Andrea fell. Everything promised well for the operations; he had brought the generals in communication with Sir Home Popham, and given the fullest instructions to the guerilla chiefs; and he considered that the time had come for his return to Corunna. He took leave of the commodore the same evening, and sailed in the *Sparrow* brig, which was proceeding to Corunna for supplies.

A few days brought him to his destination, and he received a sort of public welcome on his arrival, all the authorities hastening to pay him visits. But his activity could not be arrested by ceremony, and he was at work the moment he landed, sending off 300,000 musket-cartridges and 10,000 flints to Sir Home Popham, and starting couriers to Lord Wellington and General Castaños.

★★★★★★

Sir Howard now received from the Captain-General Castaños a letter of congratulation, a part of which is here given, translated from the original in the *Douglas Papers*:—

Santiago, 8th July, 1812.

My esteemed Friend,

In addition to what I officially communicate, I congratulate you upon the beginning of the campaign in Cantabria, in the direction of which your presence has been of great importance. It would also be of much use here, as we are in a miserable state; but without attending to obstacles we are obliged to act, in order not to lose any advantage. Providence has disposed that all our undertakings shall be attended with a happy result, which ought to augment the confidence Lord Wellington should have in his good fortune. He writes to me very contented from Medina del Campo on the 3rd

I beg you for God's sake to assist us with clothing; and trusting very soon to have the pleasure of seeing you,

I am your friend and servant,

Castaños.

★★★★★★

The Spanish corps before Astorga was at a stand for ammunition, and he forwarded a supply, and then went to see what progress had been made with the siege. He found that the troops had surmounted extraordinary difficulties, and were animated by the best spirit The obstinacy of the defence had not diminished their ardour, and he was a spectator of an exploit by the regiment of Rivera, which would have reflected honour on any troops. It became necessary to dislodge the enemy from a small rising ground where they harassed the men employed in the prolongation of the right trench, and the Rivera regiment dashed at them with the bayonet under a galling fire, and compelled them to fly. He felt proud that his anticipations had been so verified; for everything bid fair for success, as the approach was already curtained, the trenches advanced, and the guns mounted in the breaching batteries. He saw that he could be of no use for the moment, and accepted an invitation to accompany General Santocildes to Leon, to witness the proclamation of the new constitution.

The ceremony was one of grave import, and lacked no accessary that could render it imposing. Flags decorated the public buildings, and waved over the churches; the tradesmen closed their shops, and dressed them with evergreens and flowers; and loyal mottoes glittered on banners, and emblazoned the walls. Holiday crowds paraded the streets, and the windows of the houses were thronged with ladies, attended by nobles and cavaliers. The Grand Plaza was lined with troops, and rolling drums and the bray of trumpets notified the approach of the general, who role at the head of a brilliant train, composed of his staff and the functionaries of the province.

He was warmly received by the people, but they burst into acclamations at sight of Sir Howard in the British uniform, and his horse could hardly make its way through the crowd, which pressed round him on all sides, mingling his name with shouts for Wellington and England. Hats were raised aloft, and ladies waved their handkerchiefs and threw flowers from the windows. So kind a nature could not receive such greetings without emotion; but he was affected less by the people's enthusiasm than by the tokens of their affection and gratitude, not a few shedding tears as they called out the name of Wellington. On the other hand, the proclamation of the constitution occasioned little excitement, so completely were the sympathies of the nation absorbed by the war.

He returned with the general to Astorga, and charmed the soldiers by going into the trenches, exposing himself to the heavy fire for several days in succession. A despatch from Lord Wellington called him away from the siege by informing him that King Joseph had left Madrid at the head of 12,000 men, which made it desirable that General Santocildes should draw nearer the English Army; and he arranged with the general to advance on the Douro with 8,000 men, leaving a similar force to prosecute the siege. The late successes had given the people hope, as well as gratified their pride, and the troops met a joyous welcome as they pushed forward; while Sir Howard received a perfect triumph. The moment was at hand when he was to reap the reward of his efforts, in seeing their object fulfilled.

His scheme for occupying the French in the north by the expedition under Sir Home Popham, and for covering the Allied Army by the operations of the several Spanish corps and of the guerillas and Alarms, was acknowledged to have contributed to the victory of Salamanca, by keeping off Lord Wellington two divisions of infantry and one of cavalry, except about fifteen hundred sabres which were pushed forward, and joined Marmont the night before the battle.

★★★★★★

The succours thus diverted are mentioned by Napier:—"Forty-nine thousand men, of which thirty-eight thousand were with the eagles, composed the army of the north, under Caffarelli, and were distributed on the grand line of communication from St. Sebastian to Burgos; but of this army *two divisions of infantry and one of cavalry, with artillery, were destined to reinforce Marmont.*"—*Peninsular War,* vol. v.

★★★★★★

The armies engaged were so nearly equal, (the Allied Army numbered 40,000; the French 42,000—*Peninsular War,* vol. v.), that fortune might have inclined to the French if they had obtained this reinforcement, and the fruits of the campaign would have been endangered. The Spanish Army was entering Carvajales when news came of the victory, and it excited the wildest joy among the troops and the population of the surrounding country. "It caused me the greatest delight," writes Sir Howard, who had just received a letter from the Minister for War, recalling him to England. The objects for which he had laboured were attained, and his mission was at an end.

CHAPTER 19

Foils the French Generals

No one but Lord Wellington understood the position of the French in the Peninsula so well as Sir Howard, and it was from him that the Great Captain drew most of his information. He could thus appreciate the victory of Salamanca, and see what consequences it opened. The time has come when it may be stated that he took a different view of the situation from his chief. He was of opinion that Lord Wellington should have followed up the defeat of Marmont by a vigorous pursuit, which would drive his army beyond the Ebro—involving the fall of Burgos before it could be succoured by the French force in the south— and giving such support to the squadron and guerillas in the north by this advance that the enemy's line of communications with France on that side would be cut off, and Soult and King Joseph compelled to move towards the other line, and form a junction with Suchet.

Indeed, the first line was already broken, for intelligence had arrived of the fall of Castro, the siege of which we have seen Sir Howard arrange with Sir Home Popham and Longa; and he had settled with the commodore and General Mendizabal to proceed from there to Santona and Laredo. They had strictly followed his plans, and brought Santona to great extremities, so that it must fall on Lord Wellington's appearance, and the possession of St. Andrea would insure him every supply by sea. This movement seemed to result so plainly from Marmont's defeat, that Sir Howard felt sure it was what the commander-in-chief designed. But he had written to him to say that he would take advantage of the approach of General Santocildes to repair to headquarters while the Spanish troops invested Zamora, and he resolved to avail himself of any opening to refer to the position of the different armies, and deliver his opinion.

He was obliged to make a halt at Valladolid, and here he learnt how his name had spread through Spain, the notables of the town coming to pay their respects as soon as they heard of his arrival. He was most affected by a visit from the bishop, who had originally been a partisan of the French, and been rewarded by the Grand Cross; but lost their favour on refusing to issue an address in their interest. General Kellermann even seized him by the throat, and flung him out of the room, without respecting either his office or years, and the old man of eighty thought it prudent to fly, having received a hint of danger.

The incident taught him that he could not halt between two opinions, and he returned to the city a changed man, avowing devotion to the royal cause, and caring for neither threats nor cajoleries. He talked cheerfully to Sir Howard, spoke of his exertions and achievements, and eulogised Lord Wellington, whose recent victory filled every mouth. Sir Howard expressed a wish to see the works of art in the city, and he gave him an order to visit the religious houses, describing him by name, which obtained him unexpected attentions. He was in the chapel of the Bernardine convent, when the nuns heard of his presence, and went to do the honours themselves, which they did in the most complete manner, showing him all the statues and pictures, and relating their history.

The curiosities included the body of their benefactor, Don Garcia, son of the great duke, the tutor of the unfortunate Don Carlos; and he asked for a memento, expecting to receive a clip of his garment. But the nuns carried their complaisance farther, and one of the party broke off the *don's* great toe, and presented it to him in a silk purse, the work of her own hands. Yet these women felt kindly impulses—only they had so familiarised themselves with death, that they looked on inanimate forms as but clay.

They introduced him to a nun who had entered the convent in her girlhood, and unexpectedly succeeded to a vast inheritance, which led to her being taken from her noviciate, and brought out at court. There she attracted a host of suitors, and every effort was made to reconcile her to the world. But she persisted in her first intention, and was finally allowed to take the veil, leaving her property to the next heir. Her story reminded Sir Howard of the English girl whom he found amongst the Indians, and he attributed her decision to the same cause—a lethargy of feeling induced by habit.

He met as kind a reception at the Franciscan convent, devoted to noble ladies, who were obliged to prove descent from a remote period. The abbess had been celebrated for her beauty, and preserved its remains, being only in middle life; and he was fascinated by the manners of the nuns, who retained the polish of the court. They entertained him with a little concert, one playing the organ while the others sang, and then showed him round the convent. It now appeared that they possessed as great a treasure as the nuns of St. Bernard—a dead benefactor; and Sir Howard duly examined the body of the Marquis of Sule Yghsa, secretary to the Duke of Lerma, but whether the same secretary who figures in *Gil Blas* he does not mention, his thoughts being bent on obtaining another relic. It is amusing to find the nuns presenting him with a finger, which one wrenched off the mummy, perhaps to pair with his toe. To such ends do secretaries and Caesars come!

The nuns were not so out of the world as to be ignorant of what passed, and told Sir Howard they had heard of his services to their country, and what they effected. He writes in his note-book:

> They all begged me to visit them again, most particularly at Posta Cela, where they actually embraced me, and wept for joy.

He noticed a diverting result of the French occupation of Valladolid, in the games of the boys, who were all playing at soldiers, and fought battles in every street. They had begun the practice in the French time; but one day fired off toy-cannons and pistols with charges of powder, and this raised an alarm, when a guard beat to arms, and the garrison turned out before they discovered the cause. Playing at soldiers was then found to be incompatible with soldiering in earnest, and was placed under an interdict.

Sir Howard met Lord Wellington near the city, and had cause to be pleased with his reception. But he saw there was no intention of taking the course he had surmised, as the pursuit of Marmont had been given up, and Lord Wellington merely ordered him to call upon Santocildes to occupy Valladolid, in communication with the other Spanish corps and the 6th Division at Queguar. He concluded that something had arisen to divert the commander-in-chief from the forward movement, and did not regard the occasion as one on which he could speak, though his suggestions always received consideration.

★★★★★★

The march on Madrid is thus adverted to by Sir Howard in a minute on the Battle of Salamanca:—"I felt convinced that some unexpected and imminent necessity elsewhere, in directions of which I knew nothing, rendered this indispensable, and

131

it would not have been prudent—scarcely respectful—in an officer to have ventured unsolicited an opinion to the illustrious general upon matters of such high import. Many attempts were made to draw me out upon the subject; but I most carefully reserved my opinions at the time, only imparting them confidentially to one or two friends. The manner in which Marmont was brought to battle by Lord Wellington was masterly in the extreme."

★★★★★★

The pursuit of Clausel to Valladolid presented no obstacle to the advance of King Joseph, who might have formed a junction with the defeated army, and made it the superior force. He could then have prevented Lord Wellington from moving on Madrid, as well as from advancing into the north, and forced him back to the line of the Douro, if he did not compel him to retire into Portugal. But the French lost the favourable moment through the negligence of the king, and Lord Wellington's movement was unopposed. (Minute by Sir Howard Douglas on the Battle of Salamanca.)

The commander-in-chief invited Sir Howard to dinner, and spoke in a gratifying manner of his services, mentioning the large force kept off his hands by the operations on the coast, and requesting him to state this to Sir Home Popham. Sir Howard had also a long conversation with Colonel Burgoyne of the Royal Engineers, and they arranged to suspend the siege of Zamora, which he had left in progress, and only carry on that of Astorga, as Lord Wellington directed him to set off in the morning, and bring the Galician Army to Medina del Campo.

They had another conference on the morrow, when they rode away at the same time, Lord Wellington proceeding to Cuillar, where he had stationed a division of the army, and Sir Howard making for the heights of San Roman. To this place General Santocildes had advanced, and he again put his army in motion on the arrival of Sir Howard, who accompanied him to his assigned post.

Even Sir Howard's frame bent under so much fatigue, and the strain brought on an attack of fever, which confined him to bed for two days, a most untoward event, for it prevented his being present at the interview of General Santocildes with Lord Wellington. This led to embarrassment in their future intercourse, for the general treated him with reserve on perceiving that he was ignorant of his instructions, though they would doubtless have been communicated by Lord Wellington, if he had not thought that the general would report what passed, as he knew Sir Howard was to have attended the meeting. Sir Howard felt the more annoyed as he was certain the French would retrace their steps directly, they heard of the advance on Madrid, and it became important to know whether such a contingency had been estimated.

He stated his apprehensions to Santocildes, and requested information, but to no purpose, and he went to make inquiries about the enemy on the road. An orderly dragoon met him at Torre de Cilhas, with despatches, and he found his misgivings verified, for the French had crossed the Duenos, and were marching in force on Valladolid. A despatch overtook him from General Santocildes at the same time, informing him of this movement, and requesting a meeting at Villa de Fraydes to devise new arrangements. Sir Howard reached the spot at five in the afternoon, the time appointed, but the general did not make his appearance, and he waited for him through the night in great anxiety. This was relieved about four in the morning by an *aide-de-camp* from General Cabrera, who announced that the Galician Army was retiring on Castro Nuovo.

The night's harass left him very exhausted, but he rode off directly, and found General Santocildes was suffering from fever, which rendered an interview impossible. The army was in retreat, but he could elicit no information from General Cabrera, and only gathered its destination from conjecture. One of his spies came in during the night and reported that the troops pushed forward by the enemy were commanded by General Foy, one of the most enterprising of the French generals, whence it struck him that they would aim at nothing less than the disruption of the communications of the allies, and the relief of Astorga, if they did not try to recover Salamanca.

Both the Galician Army and the Portuguese force under the Count of Amaranthe were thus placed in a critical position, as General Santocildes had retreated on a line which left the communications exposed, and brought him into a country open to cavalry, in which the enemy was very strong, while the Spaniards numbered but 300 sabres. Hence, they had, no way of escape but by making for the mountains, and he went to impart his views to the general as soon as he saw the danger. The hour might seem unseasonable for disturbing a sick man, as it was but four in the morning, but the case did not admit of delay, and he proved behind time, for Santocildes had set out for the rear an hour before, leaving the troops without a commander.

Such was the position of the retreating army! Sir Howard spurred off to the Count of Belvidere, the officer next in rank, and begged him to assume the command, for all must be lost if there were any hesitation. His notes describe the count as "really a very fine fellow," and the character seems deserved; but he shrank from the command under such circumstances, and urged his infirm health and ignorance of Lord Wellington's instructions, without which he should feel paralysed. Thus, the army was without instructions or a chief, and the enemy advancing.

Sir Howard tried what could be done with General Cabrera, but found him equally unwilling; and he justly said that the command devolved on the count, and that he could not assume it over his head. Ultimately Sir Howard persuaded the count to act until orders should be received from General Castaños, and induced him to march in a direction to take up a position behind the Esla, where he would be in communication with the Count of Amaranthe and the Portuguese corps, and whence both might retreat into Portugal, if necessary.

Sir Howard informed Castaños of his conviction that the first object of the French would be the relief of Astorga; and he is proved to have been right by a minute from General Foy in later years, which states that "*l'Empereur Napoléon attachait la plus haute importance à la conservation d'Astorga.*" (Minute by General Count Foy, in reply to Sir Howard Douglas.—See Appendix.) The French advance would compel the withdrawal of the division before the town, so that the Spaniards must raise the siege or capture the place by a dash, and he exhorted General Castaños to adopt the latter course. Only a few hours remained for the work, as General Foy had reached Toro, and was approaching by forced marches; but he possessed no means of forewarning the garrison, and they had lost hope of relief.

General Castaños took advantage of their want of information, and threatened to spring a mine if they did not surrender, and they laid down their arms to find that the Spaniards had withdrawn their battering train, and formed to retreat. Thus, fell Astorga, after a two months' siege, which provokes a sneer from Napier, but unmarked by his usual judgment; for it is no reflection on the Galician Army to have been detained for this period before a town which had stood out against Junot for six weeks, resisting a powerful French Army, supplied with every equipment. Sir Howard affirms that they behaved with spirit, and that the achievement shed honour on the Spanish arms.

He left the retreating columns to visit the Count of Amaranthe, and give him the benefit of his counsel. His only companion on the journey was his secretary, and they rode through a lonely country, where he incurred some danger; for the French would pay for his capture, and were said to have adherents in this quarter. But he deemed himself safe amongst Spaniards, and felt no misgiving as he spurred along, surveying the wild scenery which there meets the eye. They stopped to dine at a roadside inn, and their nostrils caught a savoury odour as they entered, promising unexceptionable cheer. Such indications are very pleasant on the table, but tantalize in the distance, and the secretary could not bear the delay that ensued with the same patience as the commissioner, but cast looks at the door, as steps again and again approached, and again passed by.

But relief came at last, for the steps paused at the threshold, the hostess appeared, and a stew steamed on the board. Can we marvel that he fell to amain? Who would wish Sancho Panza's physician to have stood by, and laid an interdict on the dish? Yet some such caution had been well, for his knife and fork plied quick, and he was only pulled up by a qualm which took away his breath. He began to feel giddy, and started from the table, making a rush, for the door. But he fell short, and rolled on the floor in convulsions.

His discomposure escaped Sir Howard till he rose up, but he now sprang to his assistance, and called for the servants of the inn. He sank himself as they arrived, seized with the same symptoms, followed by vomiting. The secretary also became sick, and the hostess and servants looked on bewildered, neither knowing what to make of the occurrence, nor what to do. Their terror acquitted them of foul play, though this could hardly be suspected, as they were Spaniards, and Sir Howard's uniform insured good will. But they had traversed an infected district, and it was possible that some French spy had followed them to the inn, and drugged their dinner. Sir Howard learnt that a Portuguese doctor was staying in the village, and he requested the hostess to call him in, while the servants carried them to bed. The doctor promptly appeared, heard their report, and came to the same conclusion as themselves.

"They have been poisoned," he said to the hostess. The poor woman stood speechless. He turned to the servants, and repeated the words, with angry gesticulations. But they burst out in chorus, with gesticulations surpassing his own, and declared that it could not be, invoking the saints to bear them witness, and mentioning a totally different personage in connexion with the doctor. Then the hostess found words, and protested her innocence, which Sir Howard never doubted, although she did protest too much.

The clatter lasted so long that both the secretary and himself recovered during its progress, and he ended the dispute by requesting her to produce the saucepan in which the stew had been made, and satisfy herself and them by having it examined by the doctor. She readily agreed, and brought in a large copper pot, thick with *verdigris*, and it came out that the stew had been standing in it since the previous day. Their sickness was now explained, and they comprehended their recovery, for the doctor reported that the poison had supplied its antidote in the overdose.

The news of General Foy's advance drove the Count of Amaranthe across the Esla; but he resumed the blockade of Zamora as soon as he became acquainted with Sir Howard's plan for preserving his communications with the Galician Army. The two officers held a conference, and agreed in the importance of this measure; for there was a chance of capturing Zamora before General Foy learnt its danger. But Sir Howard recommended the greatest vigilance, as Foy might strike the count by cutting off his retreat instead of marching forward. Thus, he sought to guard the campaign at a moment when his mission had ceased, and he had actually received his recall, feeling the same interest in the cause of Spain, and the same zeal for its advancement.

But circumstances, were occurring to subvert his arrangements, for General Castaños had handed over the Galician Army to General Cabrera, and he instantly changed his front, directing the retreat on the mountains, though the fall of Astorga had strengthened his position, and doubled his numbers. The news met Sir Howard on his way back, and he spurred so fast after the columns that he nearly rode into the ranks of the enemy, being stopped by a peasant, who told him they were in force at Labajesa. He turned into another road, and came up with the general in the village of Tornero. Murillo would have made a picture of their meeting. The hour was midnight. The Spanish general reined up at the head of his staff, as the English officer presented himself, covered with dust, and worn with his long ride. He adjured him to suspend the retreat, and take up a position to support the Count of Amaranthe, and preserve their communications.

Cabrera replied that this could not be done without sacrificing his army, as he had no means of facing the French cavalry, which would appear in a few hours. But Sir Howard insisted that their movements showed they had no intention of advancing to Tornero in force, and that they would cut off the Portuguese corps when they heard what direction he was taking. Cabrera expressed the greatest deference for his opinion, but was unconvinced, and declined to halt.

"I will only ask you to remain here till morning," urged Sir Howard.

"I could not remain an hour," was the reply.

"Then I will remain alone."

The general rode forward, and Sir Howard kept on the spot, to the wonder of the soldiers, as they hurried past, eyeing his familiar figure, thrown up by the light from the inn. He could not but think what they might have accomplished if they had been properly led; for the siege of Astorga had shown him their quality, and he entertained the highest opinion of the Spanish soldiers. He writes to the Earl of Liverpool on this occasion:

> I must say they are well deserving of being better commanded. They really possess all the qualities necessary to constitute good soldiers. (Despatch of Sir Howard Douglas to the Earl of Liverpool, August 26, 1812.)

But such thoughts did not occupy him long; for his mind now wandered to the battalions of the enemy, and considered in what manner they would be employed when Cabrera's movement became known. Nothing could be ascertained till morning, but he had formed an opinion, and it was to test its accuracy that he incurred his present risk. He thought that it might be imprudent to remain in the village, and he established a bivouac about a mile away, though not venturing to stay on one spot, and he kept his horse ready saddled, that he might gallop off on the first alarm.

Thus, he watched through the night, and experienced no interruption, not a soul appearing on the road. Some peasants came past in the morning, and he then learnt that the French had not occupied the village, though their patrols had been seen on the other side, almost up to its entrance. He now felt satisfied that he had penetrated their designs, and that they had taken the direction he anticipated.

His perfect foresight on the occasion is susceptible of proof; for General Foy visited England in 1817, and the Right Hon. William Wickham submitted to him a Minute from Sir Howard, detailing what he conceived to have been his intentions in the advance, with a request that he would state how far it was correct. "*L'officier qui a écrit ceci a parfaitement deviné les intentions du Général de Division Comte Foy pendant les opérations du mois d'Août, 1812*," wrote the general, and he adds the details of his plan. The minute and the commentary are given in the Appendix to this volume, and form a worthy memorial of Sir Howard's sagacity.

The fact of the French having taken the direction of Tabra convinced him that their object was to seize Carvajales, and this would place them between Portugal and Zamora, cutting off the Count of Amaranthe, which led him to hurry off his orderly with a letter, begging him to be first at the point. The count acted with his usual energy, putting his columns in motion as soon as he received the despatch; and thus, saved his army. An hour later he would have been lost.

The French cavalry overtook his rear-guard near Constantina, and made a furious charge, but his dispositions were so excellent that they captured only a few stragglers, and he made good his retreat, after leading them a chase by which they lost the opportunity of dashing at Salamanca. For Sir Howard's report of their advance recalled Lord Wellington from Madrid, and Marshal Clausel summoned Foy back to Valladolid directly he heard of this movement. How different might have been the results if Sir Howard had accompanied the Galician Army in its retreat instead of passing the night at Tornero!

★★★★★★

Sir Howard was anxious to know whether the service he had rendered on this occasion was acknowledged by the Count of Amaranthe, and he made inquiries on the subject of his friend Sir Benjamin D'Urban, whose reply is dated Cintra, 10th October, 1815, and may furnish an extract:—"I wrote to the Count of Amaranthe to beg that if he had made such a report he would favour me with a copy of it, and that, if no such despatch had been made, he would send me a certificate of his having received important intelligence from you during the period in question. I enclose you his answer, which I think you will find satisfactory as an acknowledgment of most essential and valuable intelligence and service rendered by you."

★★★★★★

Chapter 20

Joins Lord Wellington

Sir Howard's mind felt lightened after sending off his orderly to the Count of Amaranthe, and he was strolling down the village, when he heard the clatter of hoots, and presently was startled by the appearance of two English light dragoons. He could hardly believe his eyes at first, but there was no doubting the blushing scarlet, or the English faces of the stalwart troopers. They recognised him as plainly and rode up in a canter, while he divided his admiration between their chargers and themselves.

"This is a strange encounter, sergeant-major," he said to the foremost. "Where are you from?"

"From General Anson at Tudela, sir," was the reply. "And I think you are Sir Howard Douglas?"

"Yes."

"I have brought you despatches from Lord Wellington, sir, which the general thought it right to send on."

"A dangerous service!" said Sir Howard, more astonished as he looked at the address on the despatch. "Is it possible you have come across the country by Valladolid?"

"Yes, sir. But I heard the enemy had come up there, and that the Spaniards had retreated. I thought it my duty to persevere in conveying the despatches; so, we made our way to Casta Contrigo, where we heard you were here, and came across."

"You deserve great credit for your conduct: I have very important intelligence for Lord Wellington, and must send you on with it."

The letter was soon ready, and the two dragoons were refreshed and at the door.

"Considering the importance of this despatch," said Sir Howard, as he gave it to the sergeant-major, "I should like you to proceed by the bank of the Esla to Constantina, and then on to Salamanca."

The sergeant-major looked dubious. "Will you be so good as to give me this order in writing, sir?" he said, after a moment's hesitation.

"For what reason?" asked Sir Howard.

"Because I shouldn't take that way, if left to myself, sir."

"Well, tell me how you managed in coming here."

"It was thought this would be a difficult service, sir, and I was picked out to do it, with leave to choose my companion. I chose this man, sir, and these horses—because I knew they could be trusted; and I settled in my own mind there'd be most danger in blundering on too fast, while certainty would be better than speed. I knew I should be safe with the people, and that the French wouldn't, so, I determined to keep in sight of the French Army."

"That was bold play."

"Yes, sir. But I knew their cavalry could only chase me in a pretty large party; for a small one would be cut up by the guerillas or peasantry; and the speed of a large party would be only the speed of their slowest horse, if they kept together and chased to a distance; so I could gallop round them with these mares half a dozen times in an hour." And he glanced with pride at the two chargers.

"Did they look after you?"

"Oh, yes, sir! I went on, and we soon fell in with them. They turned out a party of cavalry as I expected, and we gave them a good gallop. They turned, and we turned. I always drew off two or three miles at night, and went to some village or hamlet—generally to the priest, and told him what we were about. We got good treatment for ourselves and horses, and set off at daylight, sighted the French again, and let them give us a gallop. But they got to know our look after a few days, and then didn't give us much trouble."

"I'm sure I can't do better than leave such an excellent tactician to his own judgment," said Sir Howard.

"I'll carry the despatch in my own way, sir, as safely as if you'd put it in any post-office in England. That I warrant."

"I have full confidence in you. Now tell me your name."

"Blood, sir."

"And yours?" said Sir Howard to the private.

"Death," replied the soldier.

Sir Howard could not repress a smile at such a conjunction— Blood and Death! But he did not ask their names without a purpose, for he addressed a report of their conduct to Lord Wellington, and suggested that it called for some mark of approbation. This procured them both a gratuity, and Lord Wellington offered to recommend the sergeant-major for a commission, but this he declined, on grounds creditable to his modesty and good sense, and which had weight with the commander-in-chief. But Sir Howard did not attach the same importance to his scruples; and he brought the case before his friend Earl Harcourt on his return to England, the earl being Colonel of the 16th Dragoons, and interested him in the sergeant-major's favour. Mr. Blood was surprised to find himself gazetted to a cornetcy in the regiment, and rose to the rank of lieutenant, when he obtained the appointment of riding-master, and subsequently held a more lucrative post. He never knew to what influence he owed his advancement, and may first hear of Sir Howard's intervention from these pages.

Sir. Howard had no sooner parted with the two dragoons than he determined to cross the country himself, first to Villafranca to confer with General Castaños, and then to Salamanca, whence he intended to proceed to meet Lord Wellington. He had sent a despatch to General Castaños to complain of the retreat from Tornero, and also of the position in which he was placed by the conduct of General Santocildes, for this had interfered with the performance of his duties. Few could have succeeded in such functions under the obstacles he met, nor could he have prevailed himself, but for the co-operation of General Castaños and the good will of the Spanish Army and people. These proved a great support, and rendered him equal to every trial.

Opposition did not provoke him to resentment, nor jealousy to ill-temper; and he retained his dignity under the slights of General Santocildes, as under the shuffles of General Abadia; They always found him courteous and conciliatory, ready to leave himself unconsidered, but inflexible on points of duty. General Cabrera might retreat with the army, but ho would remain at his post—and he remained alone. What a protest, and what an example!

His way to Villafranca lay across the Sierra de Ochanis, a stupendous ridge, joining the mountains of Asturia, and nearly their equal in height. The Spanish *sierras* impress the most careless, even after we have seen the loftier chains of other lands, and they inspired Sir Howard with a feeling of rapture. Nothing could show more the innocence of his mind than this appreciation of nature, when he rode up fresh from his bivouac, harassed with the anxieties of his post and the toils of war. His eye caught every point of the scenery, the smallest as well as greatest, and their interest was heightened by his coming to every spot versed in its history and traditions.

To hear him talk on these subjects was thus as instructive as entertaining; for his conversation gave impressions that could not be obtained from books, and which remained on the memory, unconsciously opening glimpses of his character, and the noblest of lessons. There was a modest suppression of himself in what he said, and a recognition of others—often in the humblest rank—and a Shakespearean blending of the poetic and practical, that struck young and old. The same mind which treasured up the features of a landscape and every legend and tradition, computed the dimensions of a bridge, caught the span of a river, noted the points of a fort or position, mastered the resources of a country, and even the nature of its soil. It thus taught that the steps to eminence are observation and industry, and that even genius must be content to climb by this road, and follow it with perseverance.

Nowhere could he see nature in a more varied aspect than in the Sierra del Ochanis, which unites the sublime with the beautiful, and ranges them through manifold forms. The mountain shot up at his side till the peak disappeared in clouds, while the narrow bridle-path that led up the steep overhung a precipice, straight as a wall, and descending a fearful depth. The slightest trip would have thrown over horse and rider, yet he could not keep his eye from the plain below, which had no boundary but the sky, and spread a province as the prospect. The defile was piled with rocks, looking as though a touch would hurl them down, and sometimes almost forming a tunnel, so nearly did they meet overhead.

And here a tree jutted out from the crags, in solitary prominence, and stark to its top, as if blasted by the same eruption that had cast up the rocks. Then the pass opened with a burst, showing the mountain region beyond, with its majestic peaks sweeping far out of sight, bare steeps and slopes of the smoothest turf, ravines, torrents, and cascades, falling into a valley of perpetual verdure. Sir Howard dismounted to take in the scene, and imprint it on big memory. But even admiration of the beautiful did not carry him away from the useful, and his little pocket-book notes that he found a piece of iron-ore on the slope, and that the mountains are rich in sulphur.

The *sierra* was uninhabited, so he had to pass the night in bivouac; but he had now no apprehensions of the enemy, whose troopers could not penetrate the mountains, and he slept in security. Late in the evening of the 24th of August he reached Villafranca.

General Castaños had disapproved of the retreat from Tornero, and called General Cabrera to the rear to justify the movement, the bad effect of which was now apparent. This satisfied Sir Howard, who bore no ill-will to Cabrera, but wished to make him aware that his duty imposed a responsibility which he would not be suffered to evade. It was important that he should receive such a lesson; for the time had come when the desultory warfare Sir Howard had organised must give way to operations depending on regular troops, and he could return to England with the conviction that he had put everything in train for this change. The service intrusted to him was thus completed. Henceforward the Galician Army would be under the eye of Lord Wellington, whose authority must bear down ail obstructions, and he looked forward to the result with prophetic confidence.

His representations induced General Castaños to remove his head-quarters to Astorga, where they arrived together on the 27th, and found a sad picture of the misery brought on Spain by the invasion. Two of the suburbs of the town had been levelled with the ground to enable the French to put it in a state of defence, and the number of inhabitants was reduced from twelve hundred families to about two hundred. The Spanish trenches tore up the ground beyond the ramparts, and the interior presented nothing but shattered walls, and buildings in the last stage of ruin. The siege left more terrible relics in the works, where the bodies of the slain lay unburied; and the brutal-ising effect of war appeared in the insensibility of the passers-by, even children showing indifference.

Sir Howard mentions the fact with horror, and it is a proof of the innate goodness of his nature that it was never blunted by such scenes. Indeed, they rather made him more compassionate, and gave his sym-pathies a wider scope, enlisting them for every form of suffering. He remembers the claims of humanity in the midst of a scientific treatise, and pauses to lament that Minie bullets will aggravate wounds by dragging in tags of cloth, and that the horrors of naval combat will be increased by the use of shells. Like the Great Duke, he taught that war should be averted by almost any sacrifice.

It is natural that such a character should honour art; for art minis-ters to sensibility, and he looked for its productions wherever he went with the eye of a pure taste. Thus, he snatched a few moments in this ruined town, and his pocket-book records the result in a note of his visit to the cathedral. The structure had not escaped the havoc of the siege, and he marked the traces in wall and column, and in shivered block and cornice. But the interior showed little damage, and the war might be forgotten in its silent aisles and "dim religious light." It brought out some of the best points of Spanish architecture, and was embellished with a beautiful altar, one of the finest efforts of Gaspar Bacera. The work comprised three storeys, and these rested successively on Doric, Corinthian, and Composite columns, the niches between being occupied by figures of saints, while those of the Five Virtues stood below. The statues were of marble, nobly chiselled; and some fine low reliefs appeared in the background from the same hand.

Sir Howard left Astorga in the evening, and rode on to La Baneza, where he remained till two in the morning, and then resumed his journey. Five o'clock brought him to Zamora, but so fagged and jaded that he could go no further, and he was proceeding to one of the inns when his uniform caught the eye of the Marquis of Villagrodis as he stood at a window, and he hurried out to offer his hospitality. The servants heard his name, and it flew through the town, exciting the greatest enthusiasm—for everyone knew the part he had taken in supporting the blockade which led to the withdrawal of the French garrison, General Foy perceiving that it must surrender on his retreat.

The whole population assembled before the house, and called on him to appear, joining his name with that of Wellington; and presently he was visited by the civil authorities, who invited him to an entertainment. He found it impossible to escape, for they waited to form his escort, and marched him through the town, while the people thronged round, cheering and shouting. The entertainment comprised a repast and concert, which occupied the rest of the day, and left him very exhausted. But a night's sleep restored his strength, and he was in the saddle by daybreak, making his way to Salamanca.

Here he found troops of friends, and took up his quarters with Marshal Beresford, than whom there could be no kinder host, and at whose table he passed a pleasant evening, discussing the campaign, and both hearing and telling good stories, which it is to be regretted that he forgot to insert in his note-book. He was early mounted in the morning, and his friend Colonel Hardinge conducted him over the field of battle, so fruitful of interest to his eye. Indeed, he never passed by these practical illustrations of the art of war; and his example is suggestive to young soldiers debarred from his experience of service; for such lessons are open to all, and what he could study with advantage must to them be full of instruction.

Nor is it easy to appreciate the genius of the Great Captain till we have thus stood on one of his positions, and recalled his manoeuvres on the spot where they were executed. Sir Howard's companion knew all the incidents of the combat, and related them in the clearest manner, with a soldier's pride and grasp. He often spoke of Colonel Hardinge's description of the battle, which he characterised as a perfect representation, bringing before him the whole scene. How must he have felt at the time the influence he had exercised over the action himself, in preventing Lord Wellington from being crushed by numbers!

He made a long ride from the field to Arivalo, where he met General Churton, who told him that Lord Wellington would arrive next day, and this determined him to await his coming. It was two in the afternoon before the commander-in-chief appeared. He met Sir Howard in the friendliest manner, invited him to dinner, and directed him to remain at headquarters till further orders. He was to have another opportunity of displaying his abilities before he returned to England.

CHAPTER 21

At the Siege of Burgos

Sir Howard marched with the army in the advance on Burgos, and learnt from his friend Colonel Gordon, (afterwards General Sir Willoughby Gordon, G.C.B.), that he would probably be kept at headquarters till the movement was completed. But Lord Wellington did not make known his intentions, though they were in frequent communication, and he dined with him nearly every day. They were riding together on the morning of the 6th, when the enemy appeared in front, posted on some commanding heights near Valladolid. Lord Wellington made dispositions for attack, ordering up General Anson's brigade of cavalry, with the 6th Division as a support; and a dash at the French brought off some prisoners.

The heads of the English columns came up in succession, and marched to their places on the ridge, where their commander had taken ground, and Sir Howard expected a general action. To this he looked with the more satisfaction, as he considered a victory would restore Lord Wellington the advantages, he conceived him to have lost by not following up the pursuit from Salamanca. But the opportunities of war are moments, and must be seized as they pass, for they neither linger nor return.

No one better knew their value than the English commander; and doubtless he was now aware of any slip he had made in that operation, though Sir Howard witnesses that he may have been influenced by considerations which did not transpire. He showed every desire to seize the present opening, but was prevented from attacking by the absence of the 9-pounder brigade; and it did not arrive till late in the day, when the time for action had passed. All waited impatiently for the morning, but only to meet disappointment; for the French withdrew from the position during the night, though they still occupied the city.

Sir Howard rode forward with Lord Wellington to reconnoitre, and saw all that had occurred.

An advanced party of the 12th entered the Campo Major, and drove before it the French pickets; while their army was seen retiring across the bridge, leaving a small rear-guard in the Tree Walk. These made a rash at a smaller party of English sent to cut off their advanced men, and gave them a check, killing and wounding the foremost, and then retreated over the bridge, which was instantly blown up. The explosion shook the earth, and the fragments shot up as from a volcano, for a moment veiling the spot with smoke and dust.

Sir Howard felt alarmed for Lord Wellington's safety, as he exposed himself in an unusual manner; but he turned aside after the destruction of the bridge, and they rode into the garden of the Scots' College, on the road to Calderon, where they obtained a view of the whole French Army marching very close to the river on the opposite bank, and Sir Howard estimated their number at 17,000. They left the English in possession of Valladolid.

★★★★★★

Napier describes the recovery of Valladolid very briefly, and his account is different. He merely says, "Clausel abandoned Valladolid on the night of the 6th, and, though closely followed by Ponsonby's cavalry, crossed the Pisnerga and destroyed the bridge of Berecal on that river."—*Peninsular War*, v. Sir Howard's notes make no mention of the pursuit by cavalry, and affirm that the French held the town in the morning, as stated above.

★★★★★★

The French marshal covered his retreat by a series of movements which brought the English to Burgos, and hence he fell back upon Briviesca, in company with Caffarelli, who had joined him in time to reinforce the garrison. The appearance of Burgos greatly interested Sir Howard, and he rode forward to reconnoitre the works in the train of Lord Wellington. The castle occupied a steep hill in front of the city, and comprised a strong wall, with parapet and flanks, and the additional defence of two palisaded retrenchments, one within the other. The innermost enclosed the crown of the hill, surmounted by the castle keep, which was entrenched and casemated, and capped by a battery, named after the emperor, and commanding all around. To the north stood a hill of almost equal height, sustaining a strong hornwork, not quite finished, but closed with palisades.

Sir Howard noted every point, and looked upon the place as of great strength in relation to Lord Wellington's means; but the other scientific officers conceived a different impression, and thought the means equal to the attack. His knowledge of their opinion made him doubt his own, as he entertained a high appreciation of their judgment, and he determined to satisfy himself more fully before he expressed dissent. He possessed an old plan of the castle, which he carefully studied, and then rode out in the twilight to steal a closer view. The town, the castle, and the open all lay still in the terrible suspense before battle, and the shades of evening looked like the gathering of doom. He knew how vigilant must be the watch at such a juncture, and that ball and bullet would give no warning if he became a mark. But he threw fear to the winds, adroitly stole within range, swept round the works, and made some important observations. There was a flash from the ramparts, and the bullets whizzed past, but he had gained his horse, sprang into the saddle, and darted off.

What he had seen confirmed his estimate of the place, and he resolved to impart his opinion to his friend Colonel Robe, who commanded the artillery, and hence had a voice in the operations. He found him in conference with Colonel Burgoyne, the commanding engineer; and both officers seemed glad of his appearance, for they invited him to remain, and told him the measures they had concerted with Lord Wellington. But they represented these as definitively settled, and expressed no doubt of their success; so, Sir Howard did not feel encouraged to speak out, and reserved his opinion till Colonel Robe and himself were left together.

He then stated his belief that the proposed attack would fail, which startled his friend, and he begged him to disclose his grounds for such a conclusion. He readily complied, and showed him that the point marked for attack was the strongest part of the place, defended by three enclosures; whereas but one need be breached on the eastern front; and here he proposed to make a lodgement in the salient angle, and follow it up by running a mine from the flank under the castle wall. The directness of the plan struck Colonel Robe, and he gave it his approval, asserting that it was the only one that would succeed.

But he adverted to the difficulty of submitting to Lord Wellington a view so, different from his own, and asked if he might mention it on Sir Howard's responsibility. Sir Howard did not object, but said that he must first unfold the plan to Colonel Burgoyne, as no step should be taken without his knowledge; and he went to him at once. All who know that officer will be sure that his communication was kindly received, and he thought that it made an impression, but he came away without eliciting an opinion.

Sir Howard mingled with the staff next morning, and was chatting with another officer, when he was called to Lord Wellington, and found him in conversation with Colonel Robe. He looked grave, and Sir Howard saw that his objections to the intended operations had been mentioned.

"Well, Sir Howard, you have something to say about the siege?" he said.

"I think the place is stronger than we supposed, my Lord."

"Yes, by G——! But our way is to take the hornwork, and from there breach the wall, and then assault over the two advanced profiles."

"I would submit to Your Lordship whether our means are equal to such an attack."

"I am not satisfied about our ammunition," replied Lord Wellington.

"The enemy's guns are 24-pounders, My Lord; and we have only three 18-pounders and five 24-pound howitzers. The 18-pounders will not breach the wall, and our fire must be overpowered unless Your Lordship brings up some guns from the ships at Santander."

"How would you do that?"

"With draught-oxen as far as the mountains, and then drag them on by hand. We can employ the peasantry, and put a hundred men to a gun."

"It would take too long."

"I think the place may be captured with our present means from the eastern front, My Lord," returned Sir Howard; and he disclosed his plan, with his reasons for thinking it the most practicable. Lord Wellington made no remark. Possibly he saw the defects of his own plan, but it had been deliberately adopted, and he was not convinced that it ought to be abandoned.

The guns of the fortress had kept the English on the other side of the river up to this time, but they now effected a passage above the town, and drove in the French outposts. A force attacked the hornwork during the night, and it was carried, though with a fearful loss, its garrison breaking through the assailants, and making their way to the castle, which thus obtained a reinforcement of 500 men.

The captors of the hornwork established a lodgement in spite of the fire of the Napoleon battery, and began the construction of a first battery, and a musketry trench in its front. The men worked under a continuous shower of grape, shells, and cannon-balls, which grew more intense as they proceeded, fresh guns being directed on the spot, and inflicting a murderous loss. Sir Howard exposed himself in the hornwork to make further observations, and ascertained the weakness of the eastern front, so as to place it beyond doubt. He described what he had seen to Colonel Gordon, who reported it to Lord Wellington, and came back with an intimation that he would take an opportunity of hearing it from himself.

Sir Howard was talking with Colonel Burgoyne next morning, when Lord Wellington sent for them both, and opened the subject. He mentioned the course intended to be followed, and then reverted to the plan of Sir Howard, requesting him to state it fully. Sir Howard explained it on the chart, and further represented that the eastern wall was in a ruinous condition, which marked it as the point for attack, and that the reduction of the place would be accelerated by a flank fire from heavy howitzers on the Mary battery. He refrained from pointing out what he considered insurmountable difficulties in the other plan in the presence of the Commanding Engineer, and these apparently escaped the notice of the commander-in-chief, for he finally gave it the preference. Sir Howard notes that Lord Wellington said "he approved of my plan if mining were to be used, and expressed himself handsomely to me."

The operations were carried on at such cost of life that Lord Wellington's faith in them became shaken, and he sent for Sir Howard again on the following day, when holding a consultation with Colonels Robe and Burgoyne. He then stated his intention of shaping the attack so as to turn the church. This was an entrenched building on one of the two crests of the hill, the other crest being occupied by the castle, which swept the position. Sir Howard expressed his belief that no advance would be made by the capture of the church, and that the success of such an attack was doubtful, though it must entail a great expenditure of blood, while nothing but the breaching of the castle would reduce the place.

The capture of the church would even prove an embarrassment, the vantage being in the site; and this involved a strong occupation if it should be won, as the mere destruction of the works only imposed on the enemy the construction of others as soon as it was relinquished. He said the question to consider was, whether that point offered an opening for breaching the castle; and he gave his opinion that the operation would be difficult from there, if not impracticable, comparing the means of the besiegers with those of the besieged. His arguments elicited no observation from Colonel Robe or Colonel Burgoyne, but he so far swayed Lord Wellington that a battery was ordered to be erected on the eastern face; and his Lordship expressed his approval of the howitzer battery, requesting him to take Colonel Robe to the proper spot for its erection. They went there at once, and then separated, the colonel returning to Lord Wellington, while Sir Howard passed into the trenches.

The plan of operations was now partially changed. The left battery was continued, and a sap pointed to an outwork on the western front, with the design of trying a mine communication with Colonel Jones. Sir Howard received a visit from Colonel Robe next morning, and learnt that he had been ordered to attend Lord Wellington to the spot they had marked the day before, and that he thought the howitzer battery would be erected there. But he had no faith in half-measures, and expected little from this step alone, considering that the whole weight of the attack should bear on the eastern front, and that every other method would fail. This he had frankly stated to Lord Wellington, and there was nothing to add; so he thought it undignified to appear further. He notes in his pocket-book:

> I keep out of his way, that the professional men may not accuse me of obtruding an opinion.

Nothing could be more becoming his position than such a course, and the incident of the siege thus brings out his character as forcibly as his talents. He had seen how the place was to be taken from the first, but reserved his opinion till the two directing officers made him acquainted with their designs, and only imparted it for his friend to consider and apply. It was Colonel Robe who proposed to mention the plan as his, and he willingly undertook the responsibility, though it put him in opposition to Lord Wellington; but he saw the propriety of first unfolding the plan to the commanding engineer, and apprising him of their intention. Thus, his delicacy and honesty equalled his spirit; and we should be undecided which part of his conduct to admire most if all were not consistent.

The time had now come to "keep out of the way," and it is significant of his great self-control that he cast the situation aside, and threw himself into other thoughts. His notes present us with a sketch of the castle's history dated on this very day, and he describes the stand it made against Ferdinand and Isabella in the siege of 1476. They also tell us of a visit he paid to the cathedral, under a volley from the enemy, who fired at everyone appearing in the avenue; and he enumerates its attractions and rarities—the noble altar, the picture by Michael Angelo, the tomb of the Cid, and the banner that fell from heaven, still showing the sign of the cross, though scarcely hanging together; a proof that even heavenly textures are not enduring.

How pleasant to find him again turning from the presence of war to the sanctuaries of art, and recalling history and tradition under the cannon's mouth! Yet he did not blind himself to what was passing, and it made him wish that he could withdraw; for he saw a catastrophe approaching when his presence might be embarrassing. The operations were carried on with vigour, but without success. The sap on the west was continued towards the wall, in connexion with a mine, and an approach advanced from battery No. 1, with an inclination round the face of the hill to a kind of parallel for musketry, designed to keep down the enemy's fire.

The mine was sprung at one o'clock on the morning of the 29th of September, and effected a small breach, which was entered by a sergeant and four soldiers, composing the forlorn hope. But the storming party did not come up in support, having missed the breach in the darkness, and the men returned bleeding to the trenches. Here another attack was organized, but too late, the enemy having mustered in force, and next morning showed the breach scarped.

A despatch from Lord Liverpool reached Sir Howard at this crisis, and called upon him to return to England without delay, which was what he desired, and he rode off directly to inform Lord Wellington. He found him on the hill, watching an attempt made from battery No. 1 to reopen the breach, and directing the operation. The fire brought down a part of the wall, but it fell perpendicularly, rendering the breach more difficult, and Lord Wellington marked a site for another battery, to be erected during the night. This he ordered to be armed with the 18-pounders, and directed on the same point, arranging to deliver the assault concurrently with the springing of another mine.

The battery was begun at sunset, and briskly completed, when the guns were placed and opened. But Sir Howard's anticipations of the result were literally fulfilled, for the 18-pounders made no impression on the breach, and the enemy's heavier guns overpowered their fire, while every shot and splinter came through. It became impossible to hold the battery, and Lord Wellington withdrew the men, though this had no effect on the enemy, who did not cease firing till he had destroyed the battery and disabled the guns, one being reft of a trunnion, and the others knocked off their carriages. It was seen that he had the exact range of the spot, and the commander-in-chief ordered the guns to be removed, and a battery to be erected at another point, a little to the left. Here a more solid work rose during the night, but only to entail the same doom, for the French brought their guns into a position equally commanding, and reduced it to ruin. The professional officers now held a consultation, and decided to remove the only serviceable 18-pounder to battery No. 1, and thence open again on the breach, seconding the attack by a mine.

Sir Howard did not remain to witness the result, but Lord Wellington invited him to a conference on his taking leave, and expressed his intention of obtaining some heavy guns from the squadron, as he had recommended. Sir Home Popham sent up a supply of ammunition, which arrived most opportunely, and he hurried off two 24-pounders as soon as he received the requisition. But this was three weeks after Sir Howard had made the suggestion, and the interval gave the French army a superiority of force, allowing Caffarelli to effect a junction with Bonham. They instantly advanced on Burgos with forty-four thousand veteran troops, while the army of Lord Wellington consisted of only thirty-three thousand, chiefly Spaniards and Portuguese, so that he was obliged to fall back on the ridges of Olenos, where he awaited attack. Events intervened to prevent a battle, but the allies were compelled to retreat; and Napier tells us that their general resolved:

> Though with a bitter pang, to raise the siege, after five assaults, several sallies, and thirty-three days of investment, during which the besiegers lost more than two thousand men, and the besieged six hundred in killed or wounded.

It was in this moment of disaster that Lord Wellington recalled the counsel given by Sir Howard, and exclaimed to his officers:

> Douglas was right: he was the only man who told me the truth. (This anecdote of the great duke was related to the author by General Sir William Gomm, G.C.B.)

CHAPTER 22

Employed Home

The despatch which recalled Sir Howard to England explained the reason of that step, stating that:

> In consequence of the repeated and earnest representations made by the Supreme Board of the Royal Military College in regard to the detriment which that establishment suffers from your absence, Lord Liverpool has found himself obliged to consent, although very reluctantly, to your recall from the service in which you are employed, and which you have executed to the perfect satisfaction of His Majesty's Government. (Despatch from the Minister for War to Sir Howard Douglas, in the *Douglas Papers*.)

Indeed, the service had been executed so well that nothing remained to be done; for the mere distribution of the supplies might be left to the ordinary channels. His tact, judgment, and resolution had carried him through a mission of unusual difficulty, and achieved results exceeding the hopes of his superiors. He devoted himself to the work so assiduously that his vigilance and industry proved as serviceable as his talents, though these were continually displayed; but neither talent nor zeal would have availed without his good temper. His suavity soothed resentments, and irritation subsided before his friendly manner and natural kindness, which showed itself at every turn.

He averted jealousy by seeking to advance the cause, not himself, being willing to leave the credit to others, if he attained the object; and it was impossible to be offended with suggestions urged in a way that made them seem half our own. Nor could they be resisted by argument, for they were based on information and forethought, and objections vanished before facts. His military knowledge gave the momentum, but this arose from the same habit; for he had trained himself for action by observation and study, and by recognising the value of things which others overlooked. His memoranda present nothing more curious than the odd bits of information he has jotted down, as if he read sermons in stones, and extracted a hint from everything he saw. Thus, he exercised his perception, and brought himself to work by method, so that his instantaneous conclusions were deductions, never guesses. It is not difficult to understand how his measures were successful, when we see that they all rested on such a groundwork, that they were undertaken with determination, pursued with vigour, and carried over every obstacle and difficulty.

No man was ever more loved by his friends, and he met a warm welcome on his return to Farnham. We may be sure that Lady Douglas made a handsome report of his "boys," whom he had put on their good behaviour, and one who remembered his own boyhood did not inquire too curiously. Indeed, he looked with indulgence on little lapses whether in boys or men; and he had nothing worse to correct in his children. His leisure was devoted to imbruing them with the highest principles, and the reverence they entertain for his memory proves that it was not misspent.

But leisure he had, now little, for he received the appointment of Inspector-General of Education in 1813, while he retained that of Commandant of the Senior College, and thus stamped his impress on every officer of the day, both of the Royal and Indian Armies. Such a position brought him in contact with a number of officials more jealous of their functions than General Abadia, but very prone to interfere with his. An instance may be mentioned from his experience at Addiscombe, where he was conducting an examination of the cadets, when he received a note from the lieutenant-governor requesting him to dismiss them for parade.

He read it with surprise, but made no remark at the moment, laying it on the table till the cadet under examination had finished his proposition in mechanics. He then took it up again and read it a second and third time, too prudent to act in a way to commit either the governor or himself. There was not the least alteration in his manner as he turned to the Professor of Mathematics and said, "The lieutenant-governor wishes the cadets to attend parade, so we had better finish the examination for today."

Both the professor and cadets heard the announcement with wonder, the quick military instinct perceiving the impropriety of the proceeding, and that the governor had overstepped his authority. But Sir Howard knew that such a question could not be decided in the school-room, and was not one to set an example of defying authority, or entering on an unseemly altercation. He complied with the governor's order, but immediately brought it before the Court of Directors, with a request that the Public Examiner should always have access to the college, without any interference from the lieutenant-governor, and that he alone should be empowered to fix the lengths of the examinations, and originate alterations in the system of education.

Nor did he make the application with any wish for a personal triumph, as he had received another appointment, and desired only to leave the way clear for his successor. This object he accomplished, as the regulations he proposed were adopted, and all ground for contention removed.

He exhibited the same moderation towards the professors, and could never be betrayed into an outbreak of temper, or a want of consideration. Once he was examining the Addiscombe cadets in fortification, and illustrated his observations by reference to one of the Indian sieges, when the Professor of Fortification exclaimed:

I beg your pardon, but I had it from my brother-in-law in the service, that the case was rather different from what you state.

Such an interruption rather startled the cadets, but Sir Howard let it pass, and went on with the examination. He intended to settle with the professor in a manner that would show him he was in error, but spare him humiliation; and he took him into a private room next morning and requested him to look at some official documents, which proved that he had stated the facts. He said:

Even had I been wrong, it was neither considerate nor respectful to contradict me in that open manner during the examination. I hope that you will speak to me privately in future after the examination, if you have any remarks to make.

The most sensitive could not murmur at a rebuke so gentle. (The author is indebted for these anecdotes to the Rev. Jonathan Cape, Professor of Mathematics at Addiscombe.)

Sir Howard had not long returned from Spain when he received intelligence of the death of his cousin Charles, who had been his *aide-de-camp* in Galicia, and was killed in action almost as they parted. He severely felt the loss; for their tie of kinship had been strengthened by their fellowship in danger, and his cousin's genial character.

The remembrances he cherished are revealed in letters to his friends in the Peninsular army, begging them to gather for him what could be learnt of the captain's last moments, making inquiries about his servant, and bespeaking their care of his dog, which he desires them to send home by any opportunity. Few officers of his rank would have thought of the servant at such a moment; but he recollects the poor soldier as a comrade, and excites an interest for him in officers as distinguished as himself. No answer arrived for months, when he received one from Colonel Frazer, and the letter has such a smack of the field, that the passage on this subject claims to be quoted:—

> I fear by my silence you may have given up all hope of seeing poor Charlie's dog. I had, in truth, very little myself since, on sending to Major Rice of the 51st Regiment, to acquaint him that I had secured a passage for the poor creature, I learned that she had disappeared. However, Moore, poor Charlie's servant, luckily stumbled upon her with the 18th Light Dragoons, and a few days ago the lady was brought hither, and presented me with twelve puppies next day. I am glad to say a safe passage is secured for her through James Macleod, whose servants are taking home his horse, and will look well after poor 'Bell,' who was left in their charge the day before yesterday. Macleod sailed yesterday in the packet, and will apprise you of the arrival at Woolwich of the dog. As you made inquiries about Moore, poor Charlie's servant, I should add that the man is well, and spoke feelingly of his master. He was not, however, present when poor Charles fell.

The last shot fired by the French in this war struck Sir Howard's friend Captain Herries, (afterwards Lieut.-General Sir William Herries, C.B.), and cost him a limb. The sad intelligence was communicated by Colonel Gomm, (later General Sir William Gomm, G.C.B.), in a letter reflecting the opinions prevalent in the army on the final operations of the war:—

> Biarritz, 24th April, 1814.
>
> My dear Sir Howard,
>
> Although I have been well aware how gratifying it would be to you to receive some accounts of our poor friend Herries, in addition to the public ones, I have delayed writings to you for some days past, in the hope that the events taking place in all

other quarters would before now have obtained for us a free communication, from Bayonne; and that I should have been able to have had an interview with him before I wrote. Our governor, however, does not yet consider himself authorised to desert the Imperial cause. Official communications are hourly expected, both from the government and from Soult, which will no doubt point out his duty and his interest in terms sufficiently unequivocal to bring him to a decision: in the meantime, all hostilities are at an end.

I suppose you know the nature of Herries's wound. He was with Sir John Hope in the morning the garrison made the sortie; his leg was broken by a grape-shot, and, as I feared, has since been amputated. The last accounts we have from the town state that he is doing well, and is well taken care of. Among many other circumstances attending this unlucky business (for it might have been prevented) that have given me great concern, there is nothing that has vexed me half so much as this unfortunate blow upon poor Herries; for he is a young man that ought not to have been maimed so early in life, and by the last ball that the enemy has hurled at us; but I dare say he will bear it with much more temper than I do.

It is a pity we did not think fit to communicate to the governor the official intelligence we had received two days before of the entrance of the Allies into Paris, and all the circumstances attending it. It is to be supposed that this piece of justice (I think) towards the governor, and of policy in our character of besiegers, would have prevented a loss of about eight hundred and fifty to ourselves, and something more to the French.

The Battle of Toulouse will have given a bright close to the career of Lord Wellington. It appears to have been one of the most hardly contested actions of the whole war.

Believe me, my dear Sir Howard,
            Ever most faithfully yours,
                                    William Gomm.

Sir Howard had been anxious to obtain further war service, and pushed for employment in the Peninsula; but saw the war closed without achieving his object. The return of Napoleon from Elba, gave him new hope, and he exerted his interest to be appointed to the army in Flanders, but with the same result, the ground being taken up by more powerful aspirants. But his meritorious services were recognised at the peace, and he was nominated a Companion of the Bath, and Knight of the Spanish Order of Charles III. He subsequently received the Peninsular medal and clasps.

Appendix

TRANSLATION OF ONE OF THE ADDRESSES PRESENTED TO SIR HOWARD
DOUGLAS BY THE CHIEFS OF THE SPANISH ALARMS.

To Baron Douglas.

Sn. Esteban deribas del Sil,
4th April, 1812.

Sir,

When I was anxiously expecting to see you, Sir, in this province of Orense, in order to have the honour of paying you my respects as the most beneficent representative of the British Nation, and to present to you my Company of Alarm (in which, although you would not find military men for parade, yet you would meet with a few brave mountain *tirailleurs*, good Spaniards, lovers of their religion, their country, and their king, which they have proved at the time of the first invasion of the enemy, and are ready to do it again, if again he dared to invade us, if the nation would assist us with such articles as are necessary to render this point inaccessible), my heart was overwhelmed with grief to learn that you had returned to Corunna, and the motives you had for taking that step; my grief was increased when I announced to my companions your return, as I saw that it filled them with the same sentiments, to see their hopes frustrated, and thus deprived of the aid and protection they expected to receive from you, Sir. They expressed their sorrow to me in these very words:

'Why, Sir, should we molest ourselves with exercising and sacrificing our families and properties when we see that fortune is so very adverse to us? If till now after so many sacrifices we have not been able to advance a step, what shall we do now without them? And what can we do without arms, without ammunition, and without hopes that the generous nation who assisted us will furnish us?'

These and other such plaints which they expressed to me, filled my breast with sighs, and I could not help exposing the whole to you, adding, that if the representatives of the Spanish Nation do not take a leading part with regard to the opposition of the military in the organisation of the Alarms and their armament, this same Alarm will become a monstrosity and its enthusiasm be turned into a lamentable terror.

I have sworn with them to defend these points at the cost of my life; for this purpose we need arms of every description; my means and faculties are already sacrificed for the benefit of the country; I supplicate you, Sir, in the name of the whole, that you will assist us with those necessary articles, and may the Almighty preserve you many years, &c.

(Signed)   Br. José Rozal.

SIR HOWARD DOUGLAS AND GENERAL FOY.

The following paper was drawn up by Sir Howard on the operations of General Foy in 1812, and submitted to him on his visiting England in 1817 by the Right Hon. W. Wickham—

After the retreat of the Galician Army before General Foy, from Valladolid and Tordebaton, in August, 1812, to Benavente and La Bañeza, it was an object of extreme solicitude to me, in the then critical state of the campaign, to ascertain in time what General Foy would attempt when he should hear of the fall of Astorga; being persuaded, from his character, that he would attempt some important blow.

On Friday night, the 21st of August, I was in a small village near the Bañeza, and remained the next day near that place, after the Spanish Division, had retired from Castrocontrigo and Torneros. Having ascertained General Baron Foy's march to be in the direction of Tabra, I imagined the following to be his aim. That he would march rapidly upon Carvajales; by gaining which point before the Portuguese Division then before Zamora, he would certainly have captured that division; and as Toro as well as Zamora was in possession of the French, I suspected that, should General Foy succeed in his well-arranged plan against the Portuguese, that he would then attempt a *coup de main* upon Salamanca.

161

Lord Wellington was then at Madrid with the bulk of his force, and one division was at Cuillar. Salamanca was left with a very weak garrison, and the trophies of the victory, and was the chief *entrepôt* on the line of communication with Portugal.

Apprehending this, I sent instant information to the Conde de Amaranthe, and entreated him to raise the blockade of Zamora, cross the Esla, and get through Carvajales as soon as; possible, for that Baron Foy would certainly attempt to anticipate him upon that point.

I should very much like to know if I was right on the whole case, and how near the baron was to succeed in the part he *did execute* against the Portuguese Division.

Farnham, March 25th, 1817.

General Foy appended to these observations the following re-marks:—

L'officier qui a écrit ceci a parfaitement deviné les intentions du Général de Division Comte Foy pendant les opérations du mois d'Août, 1812. L'Empereur Napoléon attachoit la plus haute importance à la conservation d'Astorga. Cette place n'avoit des vivres que jusqu'au 10 Août, tout au plus.

Aussitôt qu'on eut acquis dans l'armée Française la certitude du mouvement de Lord Wellington sur Madrid, on résolut de se porter en avant, et de délivrer les garnisons laissées précédemment à Toro, Zamora, et Astorga. Le Général Clauzel commandoit l'armée par intérim, comme plus ancien Général de Division. Le Général Foy fut chargé de détachement, comme dans le second.

Le Général Foy proposa au Général Clauzel de partir de Valencia pour Astorga. Celui-ci, ne croyant pas que la place fut très-pressé, mit de la lenteur dans les ordres. Le Général Foy ne put partir de Valladolid avec deux divisions d'infanterie, et quinze ou seize autres chevaux, que le 17 Août, a cinq heures du soir.

Le Général Foy, passant à peu de distance de Toro, appella a lui la garnison de Toro, qui n'avoit été bloqué que par des guerrillas Espagnoles, et continua sa marche sur Astorga. Il eut le 19 sur l'Ezla, près Benavente, un engagement avec l'arrière-garde de l'armée de Galice, qu'il fut impossible d'arrêter. Le 20, à trois heures après midi, en entrant à la Bañeza, il apprit qu'Astorga s'étoit rendu la veille, et que le Général Castaños (instead of being with the army, was at Villafranca), *se retiroit en hâte sur le chemin de Villafranca.*

Dès lors l'opération principale étoit manquée. Le Général Foy voulut que son mouvement ne fut pas inutile. Il savait que la division de Milice Portugaise du Comte Amaranto était devant Zamora, faisant un simulacre de siège; il voulut l'enlever. A cet effet il se dirigea de la Bañeza sur Miranda du Douro. Il étoit impossible qu'une pareille marche restât secrète, dans la disposition unanime des habitants contre l'armée Française. Le Général Foy arriva à Tabra le 23, dans l'après-midi. Il apprit là que les Portugais n'avoient pas encore évacué Carvajalis.

Des l'entrée de la nuit du 23 au 24, le Général Foy se mit en route dans la direction de Miranda du Douro. Les troupes étoient horriblement fatiguées, et la pointe du jour le 24 l'avant-garde de cavalerie Française aperçut l'arrière-garde des Portugais, qui se retiroient en grande hâte sur Constantin. La cavalerie Française étoit mal commandée, et ne fit pas ce qu'elle devoit et pouvait faire. L'infanterie étoit à deux lieues en arrière. Le Général Foy courut avec trente ou quarante chevaux sur la colonne de Selviera, et l'attaquoit à l'entrée du Portugal, dans un pays difficile. Elle étoit assez serrée pour exiger qu'on tirât contre elle quelques coups de fusil. On ne pourroit pas courir à l'entamer avec trente ou quarante chevaux fatigués. Le Général Foy fut obligé de se contenter de quelques prisonniers faits à dehors de la colonne.

Le Général Foy arriva le 25 à Zamora, avec le projet de se porter à Salamanque, ou étoient les hôpitaux, les bagages de l'armée Anglaise, et plusieurs officiers généraux, parmi lesquels le Maréchal Beresford. Il se proposoit de marcher en deux colonnes, l'une dirigée sur Salamanque, l'autre sur (blank). C'est avec cette dernière qu'auroit été la plus grande partie de la cavalerie. Les dispositions étoient faites pour cette operation; le succès étoit infaillible; mais on eut dans ce moment des avis secrets de Madrid, desquels il résultoit que Lord Wellington alloit partir avec son armée de cette capitale pour se porter à Valladolid, et peut-être même en droiture à Burgos. Le Général Clauzel prescrivit au Général Foy de se rapprocher de l'armée. Les avis reçus de Madrid étoient fondés. Lord Wellington arriva à Arevolo trois ou quatre jours après que le Général Foy étoit arrivé a Tordesillas."

LEONAUR

ALSO FROM LEONAUR
AVAILABLE IN SOFTCOVER OR HARDCOVER WITH DUST JACKET

THE FALL OF THE MOGHUL EMPIRE OF HINDUSTAN *by H. G. Keene*—By the beginning of the nineteenth century, as British and Indian armies under Lake and Wellesley dominated the scene, a little over half a century of conflict brought the Moghul Empire to its knees.

LADY SALE'S AFGHANISTAN *by Florentia Sale*—An Indomitable Victorian Lady's Account of the Retreat from Kabul During the First Afghan War.

THE CAMPAIGN OF MAGENTA AND SOLFERINO 1859 *by Harold Carmichael Wylly*—The Decisive Conflict for the Unification of Italy.

FRENCH'S CAVALRY CAMPAIGN *by J. G. Maydon*—A Special Correspondent's View of British Army Mounted Troops During the Boer War.

CAVALRY AT WATERLOO *by Sir Evelyn Wood*—British Mounted Troops During the Campaign of 1815.

THE SUBALTERN *by George Robert Gleig*—The Experiences of an Officer of the 85th Light Infantry During the Peninsular War.

NAPOLEON AT BAY, 1814 *by F. Loraine Petre*—The Campaigns to the Fall of the First Empire.

NAPOLEON AND THE CAMPAIGN OF 1806 *by Colonel Vachée*—The Napoleonic Method of Organisation and Command to the Battles of Jena & Auerstädt.

THE COMPLETE ADVENTURES IN THE CONNAUGHT RANGERS *by William Grattan*—The 88th Regiment during the Napoleonic Wars by a Serving Officer.

BUGLER AND OFFICER OF THE RIFLES *by William Green & Harry Smith*—With the 95th (Rifles) during the Peninsular & Waterloo Campaigns of the Napoleonic Wars.

NAPOLEONIC WAR STORIES *by Sir Arthur Quiller-Couch*—Tales of soldiers, spies, battles & sieges from the Peninsular & Waterloo campaingns.

CAPTAIN OF THE 95TH (RIFLES) *by Jonathan Leach*—An officer of Wellington's sharpshooters during the Peninsular, South of France and Waterloo campaigns of the Napoleonic wars.

RIFLEMAN COSTELLO *by Edward Costello*—The adventures of a soldier of the 95th (Rifles) in the Peninsular & Waterloo Campaigns of the Napoleonic wars.

LEONAUR

ALSO FROM LEONAUR
AVAILABLE IN SOFTCOVER OR HARDCOVER WITH DUST JACKET

OFFICERS & GENTLEMEN *by Peter Hawker & William Graham*—Two Accounts of British Officers During the Peninsula War: Officer of Light Dragoons by Peter Hawker & Campaign in Portugal and Spain by William Graham .

THE WALCHEREN EXPEDITION *by Anonymous*—The Experiences of a British Officer of the 81st Regt. During the Campaign in the Low Countries of 1809.

LADIES OF WATERLOO *by Charlotte A. Eaton, Magdalene de Lancey & Juana Smith*—The Experiences of Three Women During the Campaign of 1815: Waterloo Days by Charlotte A. Eaton, A Week at Waterloo by Magdalene de Lancey & Juana's Story by Juana Smith.

JOURNAL OF AN OFFICER IN THE KING'S GERMAN LEGION *by John Frederick Hering*—Recollections of Campaigning During the Napoleonic Wars.

JOURNAL OF AN ARMY SURGEON IN THE PENINSULAR WAR *by Charles Boutflower*—The Recollections of a British Army Medical Man on Campaign During the Napoleonic Wars.

ON CAMPAIGN WITH MOORE AND WELLINGTON *by Anthony Hamilton*—The Experiences of a Soldier of the 43rd Regiment During the Peninsular War.

THE ROAD TO AUSTERLITZ *by R. G. Burton*—Napoleon's Campaign of 1805.

SOLDIERS OF NAPOLEON *by A. J. Doisy De Villargennes & Arthur Chuquet*—The Experiences of the Men of the French First Empire: Under the Eagles by A. J. Doisy De Villargennes & Voices of 1812 by Arthur Chuquet .

INVASION OF FRANCE, 1814 *by F. W. O. Maycock*—The Final Battles of the Napoleonic First Empire.

LEIPZIG—A CONFLICT OF TITANS *by Frederic Shoberl*—A Personal Experience of the 'Battle of the Nations' During the Napoleonic Wars, October 14th–19th, 1813.

SLASHERS *by Charles Cadell*—The Campaigns of the 28th Regiment of Foot During the Napoleonic Wars by a Serving Officer.

BATTLE IMPERIAL *by Charles William Vane*—The Campaigns in Germany & France for the Defeat of Napoleon 1813-1814.

SWIFT & BOLD *by Gibbes Rigaud*—The 60th Rifles During the Peninsula War.

LEONAUR

ALSO FROM LEONAUR
AVAILABLE IN SOFTCOVER OR HARDCOVER WITH DUST JACKET

ESCAPE FROM THE FRENCH *by Edward Boys*—A Young Royal Navy Midshipman's Adventures During the Napoleonic War.

THE VOYAGE OF H.M.S. PANDORA *by Edward Edwards R. N. & George Hamilton, edited by Basil Thomson*—In Pursuit of the Mutineers of the Bounty in the South Seas—1790-1791.

MEDUSA *by J. B. Henry Savigny and Alexander Correard and Charlotte-Adélaïde Dard* —Narrative of a Voyage to Senegal in 1816 & The Sufferings of the Picard Family After the Shipwreck of the Medusa.

THE SEA WAR OF 1812 VOLUME 1 *by A. T. Mahan*—A History of the Maritime Conflict.

THE SEA WAR OF 1812 VOLUME 2 *by A. T. Mahan*—A History of the Maritime Conflict.

WETHERELL OF H. M. S. HUSSAR *by John Wetherell*—The Recollections of an Ordinary Seaman of the Royal Navy During the Napoleonic Wars.

THE NAVAL BRIGADE IN NATAL *by C. R. N. Burne*—With the Guns of H. M. S. Terrible & H. M. S. Tartar during the Boer War 1899-1900.

THE VOYAGE OF H. M. S. BOUNTY *by William Bligh*—The True Story of an 18th Century Voyage of Exploration and Mutiny.

SHIPWRECK! *by William Gilly*—The Royal Navy's Disasters at Sea 1793-1849.

KING'S CUTTERS AND SMUGGLERS: 1700-1855 *by E. Keble Chatterton*—A unique period of maritime history-from the beginning of the eighteenth to the middle of the nineteenth century when British seamen risked all to smuggle valuable goods from wool to tea and spirits from and to the Continent.

CONFEDERATE BLOCKADE RUNNER *by John Wilkinson*—The Personal Recollections of an Officer of the Confederate Navy.

NAVAL BATTLES OF THE NAPOLEONIC WARS *by W. H. Fitchett*—Cape St. Vincent, the Nile, Cadiz, Copenhagen, Trafalgar & Others.

PRISONERS OF THE RED DESERT *by R. S. Gwatkin-Williams*—The Adventures of the Crew of the Tara During the First World War.

U-BOAT WAR 1914-1918 *by James B. Connolly/Karl von Schenk*—Two Contrasting Accounts from Both Sides of the Conflict at Sea D uring the Great War.

www.ingramcontent.com/pod-product-compliance
Lightning Source LLC
Chambersburg PA
CBHW021109090426
42738CB00006B/567